The Mysteries of Animal Life

AGS

by
Rick Shipley

AGS®
American Guidance Service, Inc.
4201 Woodland Road
Circle Pines, MN 55014-1796
1-800-328-2560

Experiences in Science

Printed in the United States of America

ISBN 0–7854–0969–6 (Previously ISBN 0–88671–956–9)

Order Number: 90890

A 0 9 8 7 6 5 4

Contents

Introduction: Characteristics of Living Things

What determines whether or not something is alive? The answer to this question is more complicated than it may first appear. For example, many people assume that a living thing must be able move around on its own. However, some life forms rely on forces such as water, wind, or other creatures for movement. A close look at a variety of living things shows that they share some important characteristics.

Scientists do not agree on any one definition of life, but certain life processes can be seen in almost all living things. The following life processes are found in organisms of all sizes, from the tiniest single-celled creature to the largest animals on earth.

- **Metabolism**—chemical processes that change food into energy, including the processes of respiration, digestion, and excretion
- **Growth**—increase in body size
- **Movement**—motion of an entire organism or the substances inside an organism
- **Responsiveness**—response to stimuli (for example, gravity and light cause roots, stems, and leaves to respond differently)
- **Adaptation**—ability to change in order to survive in an environment
- **Reproduction**—duplication of an organism

Many scientists think that life is the natural result of certain physical or chemical conditions. For this reason, they believe that life may exist on other planets. The National Air and Space Administration (NASA) has conducted experiments to see whether any life processes exist on Mars. No proof has been found, but experiments continue.

The purpose of this book is to examine the features of animals found in the United States. The observation activities found throughout the book require the collection of the animals being studied. When studying individual creatures, be sure to treat them gently and with care. Return them to their natural habitat when the study is over.

The organisms discussed in this book are presented according to increasing body complexity. In nature, no creature is good or bad. Creatures exist because they have a job to perform. These jobs, or niches, are discussed throughout the book.

What life processes are shown in the illustration? List them in the space provided.

REVIEW

Book Review

Each kind of animal below is the subject of a lesson in this book. At the end of each lesson, return to this page and briefly describe what you've learned about the life processes listed.

1. Earthworm

Metabolism
Responsiveness

2. Arachnids

Growth
Movement

3. Crustaceans

Responsiveness
Adaptation

4. Millipedes and **Centipedes**

Movement
Responsiveness

5. Insects

Metabolism
Reproduction

6. Amphibians

Growth
Reproduction

7. Reptiles

Adaptation
Reproduction

8. Birds

Adaptation
Movement

9. Mammals

Metabolism
Reproduction

The Earthworm

Segmented, Slimy, and Industrious

Earthworms are not very popular animals. Some people find them dirty, disgusting, and unpleasant. However, earthworms are specialized creatures that have an important role to play in nature.

Earthworms are one **species** of **segmented** worms. Most of the more than 8,000 species of segmented worms live in an aquatic (water) **environment.** The earthworm, however, lives in a terrestrial (land) **habitat.** In parts of Australia, certain earthworms can grow to a length of about 3 meters (10 feet). The common earthworm looks and feels very much the same as its giant "cousin," and both kinds of worms eat similar foods.

What Do Earthworms Do?

Every living creature has a job to perform during its lifetime. This job is called a niche. The earthworm's niche is **burrowing,** which improves the earth's soil.

During the warmer parts of the year, earthworms eat their weight in soil and food each day. When they release their **castings,** or waste products, they leave behind small deposits of **enriched** topsoil. In addition, the worm's tunnels permit oxygen and carbon dioxide to circulate underground. The tunnels also allow rainfall to penetrate the soil more easily.

Scientists estimate that a hectare of typical farmland contains over 100,000 earthworms. This number of worms can turn over about forty tons of topsoil per hectare each year, which helps the land yield greater crops.

In order to tunnel, the earthworm eats its way through the soil. The plant and animal material found in the soil provides nutrition for the earthworm. Since earthworms have no teeth, they cannot chew. Instead, the soil particles they consume, which are really bits of rock, grind foods into a fine, pasty substance that can be digested.

Common Questions and Answers about the Earthworm

- **Why are worms visible after rain?**
  During and after heavy rains, many worms are found lying in gutters, on streets, and on sidewalks. Their burrows fill with water when it rains and the worms cannot breathe. They come to the surface to avoid drowning.
- **How do worms breathe?**
  Earthworms have no lungs or gills to absorb oxygen. Instead, worms absorb oxygen directly through their skin. The worm has many **mucous glands** around its body to keep the skin moist. These mucous glands are what makes the worm feel slimy. The moisture aids the intake of oxygen and helps the worm burrow through the earth.

UNIT 1

- **Do worms like the sun?**
  Most of the segments that make up the worm's body have special nerve **cells.** These cells are very sensitive to light, especially ultraviolet light. Since ultraviolet light can kill an earthworm, these cells serve as a warning system and discourage worms from remaining above ground on sunny days.

- **How do worms reproduce?**
  Nature has provided earthworms with an interesting reproductive system. Individual earthworms are neither male nor female—they are both! Animals that have both male and female reproductive organs are called hermaphrodites. However, each earthworm needs a partner in order to reproduce. Earthworms mate at night during the summer months, and they usually mate above ground. Mating frequently happens after a rain shower, when worms leave their burrows. After mating, each worm has fertile eggs to lay. The eggs are **encased** in a **mucus cocoon.** This mucus cocoon is produced by the part of the worm's body called the clitellum. The clitellum, which looks like a saddle, is located near the middle of the worm's body. The ringlet of eggs in the mucus cocoon gradually slides forward over each segment of the worm's body until it slips over the worm's head and is deposited in the soil. Each egg cocoon releases many tiny worms.

- **Where do worms go in cold weather?**
  During the winter, worms that live in the cold habitats burrow themselves several feet down into the soil, below the frost line. They remain there, inactive, until warmer weather returns.

- **Can people eat worms?**
  Although fish, birds, and moles eat earthworms, worms sometimes have **parasites** that can be harmful to humans.

Answer the following questions in complete sentences.

1. Where do terrestrial creatures live? ____________________

2. Give an example of an aquatic environment. ____________________

3. Why are earthworms unusual when compared to other segmented worms? ____________________

4. How are common segmented earthworms similar to the giant worms of Australia? ____________________

5. What is the earthworm's niche in nature? ____________________

UNIT 1

6. How much soil can 100,000 earthworms turn over in one year? ______

7. Are there more or less than a million earthworms in a hectare of farm land? ______

8. How does the worm manage to grind its food? ______

9. List three contributions that earthworms make.

a. ______

b. ______

c. ______

10. Why is too much water hazardous to the earthworm? ______

11. How do worms breathe without lungs? ______

12. Why do earthworms tend to stay underground during the daytime? ______

13. Why are earthworms slimy? ______

14. Why are earthworms considered to be hardworking? ______

15. Identify three dangers that earthworms face.

a. ______

b. ______

c. ______

16. Why do farmers value earthworms? ______

17. What is special about the earthworm's reproductive system? ______

U N I T 1

• Investigate—*Earthworm Habitat* •

Materials

2 or 3 worms
water
1 gallon jar
plastic wrap
soil (potting or garden)
large rubber band
grass clippings
black construction paper
ruler with centimeter scale
balance

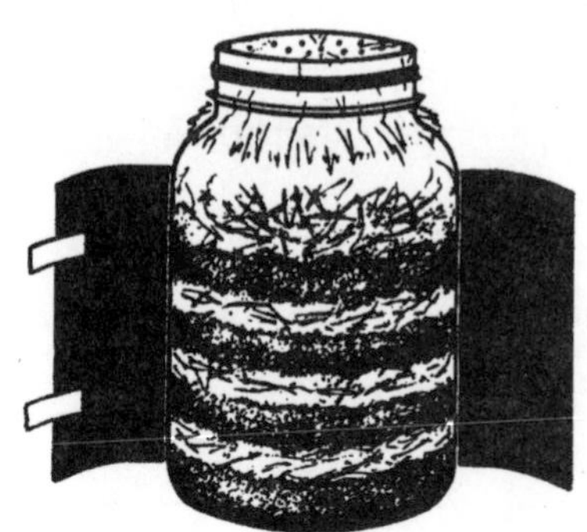

Procedure

1. Fill the bottom of the jar with about 2 centimeters (0.8 inch) of soil.
2. Add a 2-centimeter layer of grass clippings over the soil.
3. Cover the grass with 2 centimeters of soil. Continue alternating layers until there are four layers of each. Each layer should be about 2 centimeters deep.
4. Add water to make the soil slightly moist. *Do not make the soil soggy.* The worms will not survive in soggy soil.
5. Collect 2 or 3 worms. Look for them in moist soil, under damp leaves, rocks, or logs. If you can't find any worms, purchase them at a bait shop.
6. Measure the mass and length of each worm. Record that information in the data table.

Worm Statistics						
	at Start		15 days later		30 days later	
Specimen	mass	length	mass	length	mass	length
Worm A	g	cm	g	cm	g	cm
Worm B	g	cm	g	cm	g	cm
Worm C	g	cm	g	cm	g	cm

7. Examine the worms. Compare their features to the illustration.

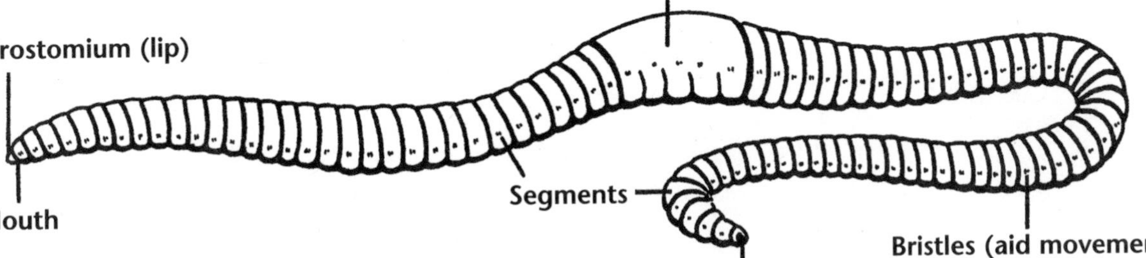

Clitellum
Prostomium (lip)
Segments
Mouth
Bristles (aid movement)
Anus

8. Add worms to the habitat you've created. Seal the jar with plastic wrap and a large rubber band.
9. Use a sharpened pencil to punch about ten small air holes into the plastic wrap.
10. Wrap the jar with black construction paper. Tape it in place.
11. Place the habitat in a cool, dark place.
12. Clean up your area if necessary. Wash your hands thoroughly.

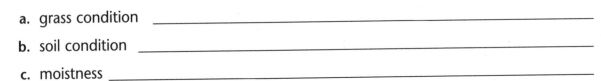

Observations

1. Remove the black covering from the jar 15 days after starting this activity. Look at the contents of the habitat. Describe each of the following:
   a. grass condition ______________________________
   b. soil condition ______________________________
   c. moistness ______________________________
   d. tunnels ______________________________
   e. color changes ______________________________
2. Carefully locate your earthworms. Describe the condition of each one.

____
____
____
____

3. If any of your worms died, explain what conditions may have caused the habitat to be an unsuccessful environment.

____

____

4. Complete the Worm Statistics chart on page 10. Repair the worm habitat if necessary.
5. The internal structure of a worm is illustrated below. Refer to the text or the glossary for a definition of any parts unfamiliar to you. Color code the following sections with colored pencils or fine-point markers:
   a. Two major blood vessels: RED
   b. **Esophagus:** ORANGE
   c. **Crop:** GREEN
   e. **Intestine:** ORANGE
   f. Male reproductive organs: BLUE
   g. Female reproductive organ: YELLOW

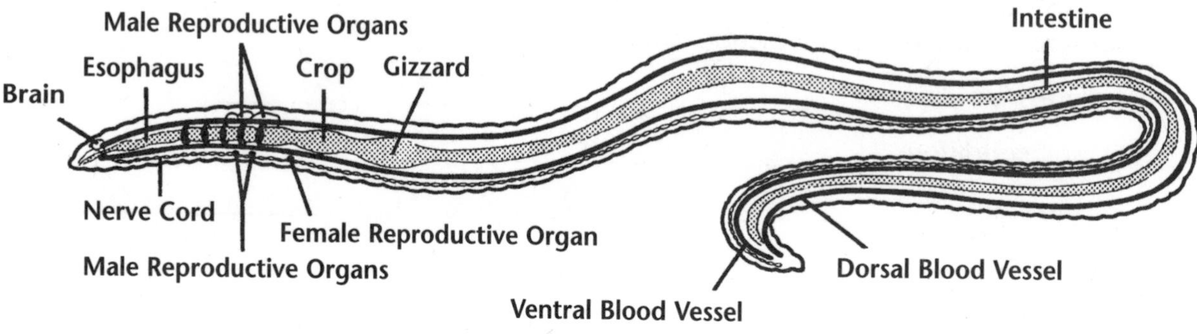

Note: In addition to the parts identified above, the earthworm has several muscle layers, mucous and digestive glands, light-sensitive cells, nephridia (which function as kidneys), and many **sensory, associative,** and **motor nerves.** Compared to many other animals, the earthworm is a complex creature.

Summary

Review the illustrations and information about the earthworm. Then write a summary explaining some of the qualities that characterize the earthworm.

Arthropods

Armor in Motion

The term arthropod refers to a group of animals that have jointed legs. There are more species in the arthropod group than in all the other groups of animals combined. The word *arthropod* comes from the Greek words *arthro,* which means "joint," and *pod,* which means "foot." Millipedes, centipedes, insects, lobsters, and crabs all belong to the arthropod group.

The arthropods discussed in this book can be found in most parts of the United States. These animals all have similar anatomical features (body parts) and physical **processes.**

Scientists believe that arthropods were the first group of animals to have a **skeleton.** This skeleton is called an exoskeleton because it is on the outside of the body. The exoskeleton offers protection from some **predators** (hunters) and seals in the animal's body moisture. It also supports the arthropod's body, like the metal framework supports the engine of a car. Some arthropods, such as lobsters, barnacles, and crabs, have hard exoskeletons. Other arthropods, such as flies and moths, have softer exoskeletons. The hardness or softness of the exoskeleton depends on the amount of lime (calcium carbonate) the animals contain. Greater amounts of lime cause a harder skeleton.

An exoskeleton does not **expand** as an animal grows. This means that as arthropods get bigger they must molt, or shed their outer shell. Some animals molt more than a dozen times in their life span.

Molting is a complicated process. The procedure involves the secretion (giving off) of a molting fluid. This fluid detaches the exoskeleton from the body of the animal. Underneath the old, detached skeleton, a soft, new one begins to grow. In order to split the old shell open and stretch the new shell to a large enough shape, the creature expands its body by swallowing air or water. Then the animal crawls out of its old exoskeleton and hides until its soft outer tissues harden once again. While its new exoskeleton is still soft, the arthropod is at great danger from predators.

Spiders, Mites, Ticks, and Scorpions

The group of arthropods called **arachnids** includes spiders, mites, ticks, and scorpions. The name arachnids comes from a Greek legend. According to the legend, there once was a young maiden named Arachne, who was a great weaver. She was so proud of her weaving that she challenged the goddess Athena to a weaving contest. When Arachne wove perfectly, Athena got angry and turned the maiden into a spider so that she could only weave webs.

Spiders

Although some spiders, such as the brown recluse and the black widow, are dangerous to humans, many people are more afraid of spiders than they need to be.

Most spiders, including the tarantula, are harmless to most people. In fact, spiders are very helpful to humans. Their niche is to control insect populations, and they eat many harmful insects. They eat grasshoppers and lizards, which destroy crops, and they eat flies and mosquitoes, which spread disease.

All spiders spin silken fibers. The spider creates these fibers by producing fluids from a series of **spinnerets** located on the back of the abdomen. When these fluids come in contact with air, they harden and form a silklike substance. The silk is used to weave webs, wrap around **prey,** and protect the eggs laid by the spider. Wherever a spider goes, it spins a silk thread behind itself.

Not all spiders weave webs, but many of them do. A spider uses both sticky silk and dry silk to weave a web. A spider doesn't stick to its own web because it knows which strands are safe to walk upon.

A spider was taken into space and observed on the giant Sky Lab space station. Scientists wanted to see if it could weave its web in zero gravity. At first, the web was **haphazard** in appearance. In time, the spider learned to produce a normal-looking web.

Spiders that do not spin webs hunt for their prey. They may chase insects or lie in wait and pounce on them. The trapdoor spider, for example, waits underground until it senses the presence of a potential meal. Then it springs open its trapdoor and grabs its prey. Hunting spiders **paralyze** their prey with a **venom.** Then they draw out the body fluids of their victim, leaving the empty shell behind.

UNIT 2

Review

A Check in science books, on the World Wide Web, or in encyclopedias to locate information about black widow spiders and brown recluse spiders. Then write a short report explaining how to identify a black widow spider and a brown recluse spider.

B Museums and private collectors have found a convenient way to collect spider webs. Use the following procedure to collect a web of your own.

1. Find a spider web that is stretched between bushes or the leaves of a plant.
2. Locate the spider and gently coax it off the web with a small twig.
3. Spray the web with a light coating of white or black paint.
4. Slip a piece of tagboard of contrasting color behind the web and slowly bring it forward until the web adheres to the surface.
5. Place in a picture frame—a natural work of art. (**Note:** Three-dimensional webs may need to be mounted in a paper box.)

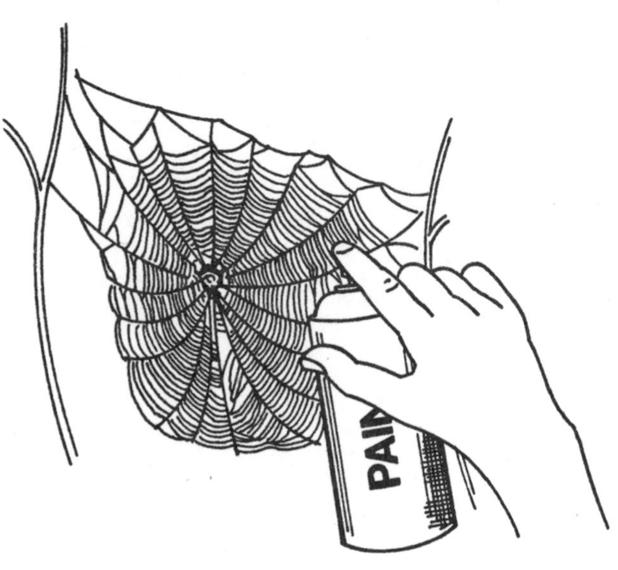

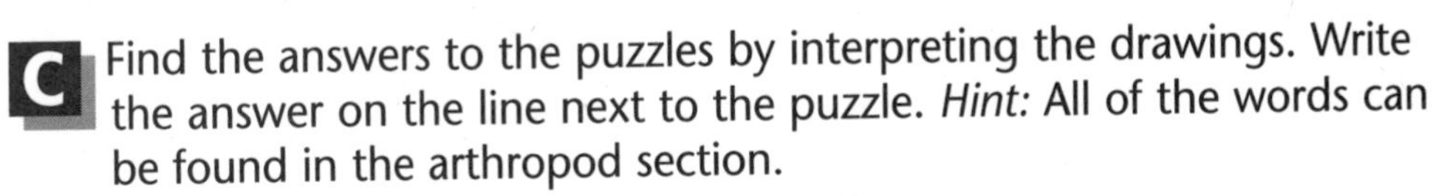

C Find the answers to the puzzles by interpreting the drawings. Write the answer on the line next to the puzzle. *Hint:* All of the words can be found in the arthropod section.

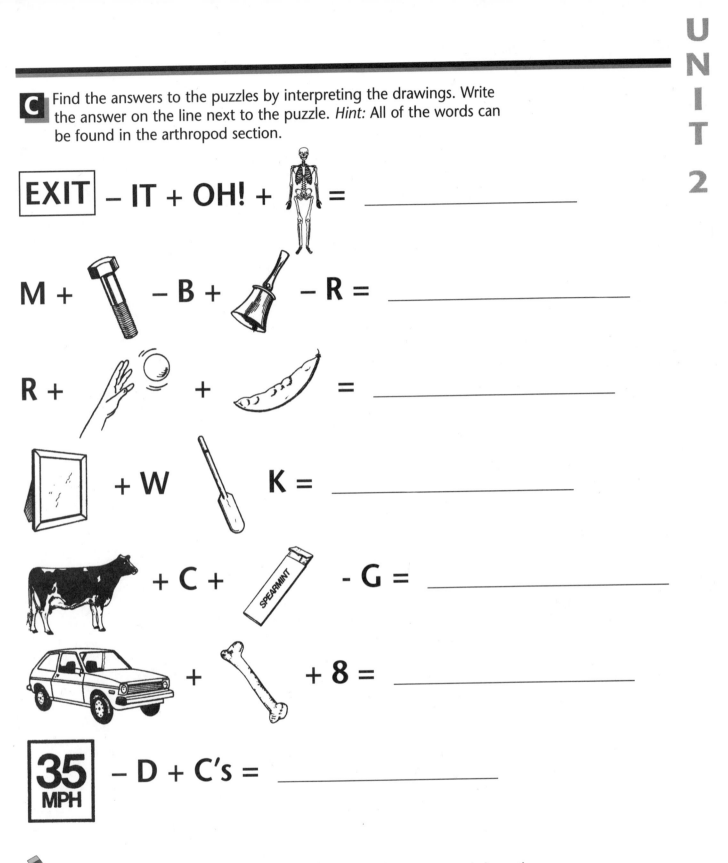

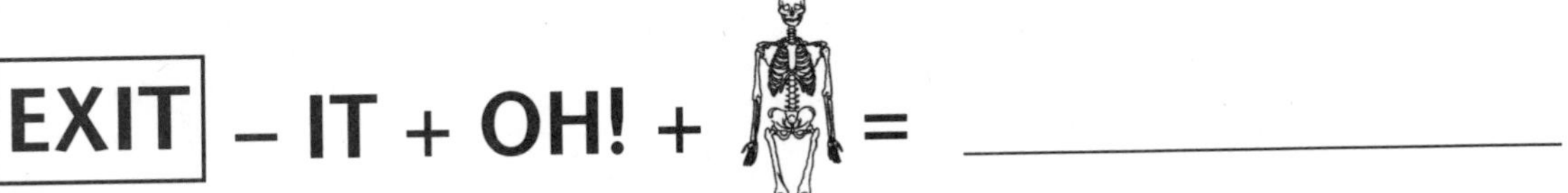

EXIT – IT + OH! + = ____________________

M + – B + – R = ____________________

R + + = ____________________

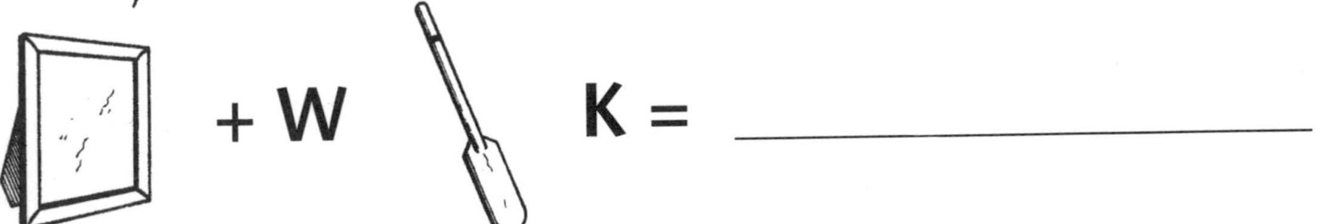

+ W K = ____________________

+ C + - G = ____________________

+ + 8 = ____________________

– D + C's = ____________________

Create your own picture-letter puzzles for science terms and share them with your classmates.

UNIT 2

Mites, Ticks, and Scorpions

Mites

These eight-legged creatures are similar in appearance to a spider, but they are much smaller. A small red mite is about the size of the period at the end of a sentence. Mites range in size from 0.5 millimeter ($\frac{1}{50}$ inch) to about 6 millimeters ($\frac{1}{4}$ inch). Unlike spiders, some mites are **herbivores.** Other kinds of mites are **parasites** that live off other creatures.

Mite

Ticks

These eight-legged animals come in a variety of species. All species of ticks are parasites. Some ticks only feed on **mammals,** and they cause a number of diseases. Rocky Mountain spotted fever and Lyme disease are especially dangerous to humans. The organisms that pass on tick-related diseases can live in a tick's body for a long time.

Ticks cling to their hosts (their source of food) with claws. Their mouths pierce the skin and draw blood. Ticks are larger than mites, but scientists categorize the two groups together.

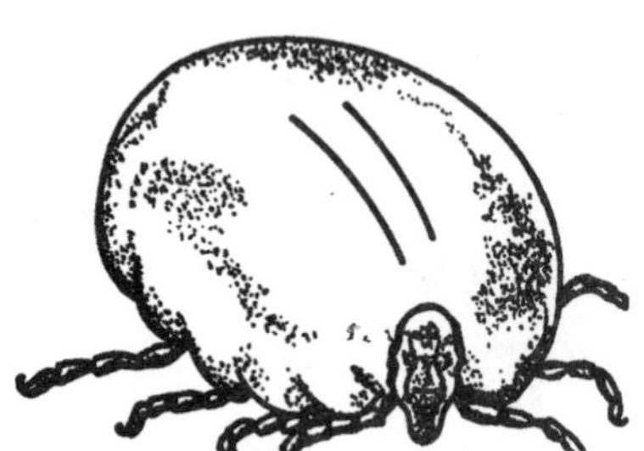

Tick

Scorpions

Scorpions, like spiders, mites, and ticks, have eight legs. They are usually black or yellow in appearance and can grow to about 20 centimeters (8 inches) in length. Most scorpions live in warm climates. However, one species is found as far north as Medicine Hat in Alberta, Canada.

Scorpions feed upon large insects and spiders. Most scorpions use a stinger in their tail to inject their prey with venom. They usually do their hunting at night. Like their "cousin" the spider, they suck the body juices out of their prey. Although scorpion stings can be very painful to humans, they are rarely fatal. Discomfort from a scorpion sting can be relieved by covering the injured area with ice and by bathing it with ammonia.

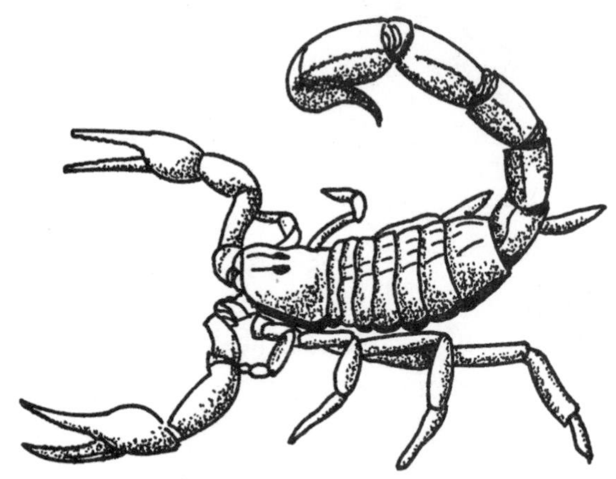

Scorpion

Unlike spiders, mites, and ticks, which reproduce by releasing many eggs, scorpions bear their young alive. A mother scorpion will carry her young for several days before letting them fend for themselves.

UNIT 2

Review

A Answer the following questions in complete sentences.

1. What kinds of animals are considered to be arthropods?

2. How is the exoskeleton useful to some animals?

3. Why do arthropods molt their exoskeletons?

4. Why is the molting process a dangerous time for arthropods?

5. What characteristics do spiders, mites, ticks, and scorpions have in common?

B List the life processes that arachnids display.

C Check in encyclopedias, books, and biology books and on the World Wide Web for information about spiders. Organize your information on note cards. Then write a short paragraph describing how spiders breathe.

Crustaceans

A Far-Out Skeleton

Crab

Crustaceans appear to have been the first arthropods. Scientists who study fossils estimate that crustaceans have been around for about 600 million years. The salty ocean is an excellent environment for preserving the remains of living things. In fact, most of the **fossil record** of life on earth comes from areas that are, or once were, underwater, which is where most crustaceans live.

Basic Characteristics of Crustaceans

- Crustaceans have jointed legs and exoskeletons.
- All crustaceans have two pairs of antennae and most breathe with gills.
- The eyes of crustaceans may be at the level of the exoskeleton or they may be at the ends of stalks. Some species can only determine the presence of light. Species that have eyes on stalks, such as crabs, crayfish, and lobsters, have better vision. The stalks can be lengthened or shortened to improve their vision. These crustaceans see movement very well. They can also see in dim light.
- The nervous systems of crustaceans are well developed. Nearly all crustaceans (with the exception of barnacles) have many bristles extending from their exoskeletons. These bristles are sensitive to taste and touch.
- All crustaceans reproduce by laying eggs.
- Lost legs and antennae are regenerated, which means they grow back if they are lost or damaged. A lost eye is often replaced by another antennae.

For many years, scientists categorized all animals that had hard, flexible exoskeletons as crustaceans. This classification was confusing because it described most arthropods. To distinguish between true crustaceans and other arthropods, a decision was made to use the term "crustacean" to identify a more specific group of animals.

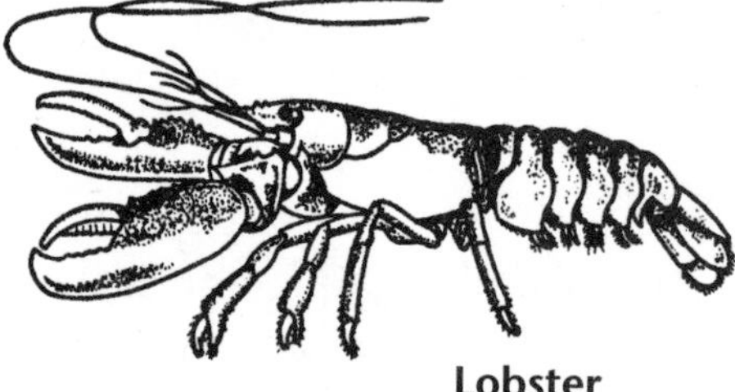
Lobster

Today, crustaceans include arthropods that have two pairs of antennae and that usually breathe with a gill structure. Barnacles, shrimp, crabs, lobsters, crayfish, and sow bugs are all crustaceans.

Most crustaceans are saltwater creatures. They've had little need to adapt over the years because the marine (saltwater) environment does not change much. The great size of the ocean keeps the salt concentration, temperature, and oxygen levels all fairly constant. However, human pollution can threaten this stable environment.

Barnacle

A few species of crustaceans live in freshwater. The freshwater environment changes drastically with each rainstorm, drought, or change of season. Crustaceans that live in this changeable setting have to adjust to the new conditions in order to survive.

Even fewer crustaceans live on land. The terrestrial (land) environment is challenging for crustaceans to survive in because it is dry. Crustaceans breathe with gills. They must keep their gills moist in order for oxygen to pass through the walls of tiny blood vessels and into their bloodstream. The gills of crustaceans such as land crabs, some hermit crabs, and sow bugs need only a small amount of moisture to function, so these species are able to live on land.

The Importance of Crustaceans

Crustaceans are an important food source for humans all over the world. Crustaceans that can be bought in stores or markets, such as crab, shrimp, and lobster, are known **commercially** as shellfish.

Crustaceans are also important to the **food chain** of fish. All fish depend on crustaceans for food during at least one stage in their development. Some fish feed upon the small **larval** forms of crustaceans. Others may eat the tiny adult forms known as **plankton** that drift about in water. Still others eat the larger adult species. Bass, for example, eat mature crayfish.

Answer the following questions in complete sentences.

1. How are crustaceans different from most other arthropods?____________________

2. Why are crustaceans considered a successful animal form?____________________

3. In what type of environment do most crustaceans live? Why? ____________________

4. What information suggests that crustaceans are an important food source? ____________

Crayfish and Sow Bugs

Crayfish: A Fish That Is Not a Fish

There are several species of crayfish in North America. A crayfish looks like a smaller version of a lobster. Crayfish seldom grow longer than 15 centimeters (6 inches). The crayfish lives in freshwater streams and ponds, while its "cousin," the lobster, lives in saltwater.

A crayfish's tail contains strong swimming muscles. When startled, a crayfish swims backwards very rapidly. This often clouds the water with material from the stream bottom, which makes it easier for the crayfish to escape danger.

One specifies of crayfish, the chimney crayfish, can tolerate long stays out of water. This unique crustacean builds a chimneylike nest in fields often far from its home stream. It burrows into the ground until it reaches a moist layer of soil that will keep its gills wet. This burrowing procedure is also used by other species of crayfish in order to survive drought conditions.

All species of crayfish have similar feeding habits. They are hunters and scavengers and eat small fish, snails, tadpoles, salamanders, worms, dead animals, and occasionally each other. Their niche is to thin out populations of old, sick, and weak animal species. As scavengers, their job is to help keep the environment clean.

Sow Bug: A Bug That Is Not a Bug

Despite the fact that the sow bug is neither a bug nor a louse, it belongs to a group called "wood lice." Sow bugs are actually crustaceans. This little animal is remarkable because it is one of the few crustaceans that lives on land.

Sow bugs, also called pill bugs or tumble bugs, can be found in almost any damp environment. They live in moist areas under stones, logs, piles of leaves, around building foundations, and even in basements. These harmless, brown animals are convenient to study. They have seven pairs of legs, all of which look exactly alike. Scientists describe sow bugs as isopods (equal legs).

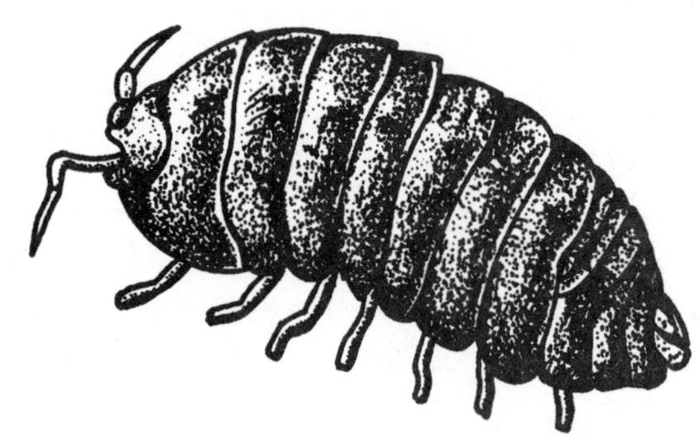

Sow Bug

• Investigate—*Crayfish* •

UNIT 2

If you live near a clean stream, you will probably be able to catch a few crayfish for study. Crayfish can also be purchased at a bait store, since many fishers use them for bait.

To create a temporary crayfish environment, put some sand and a few large rocks in the bottom of an aquarium. Fill the aquarium with aged (one-day-old) tap water. Filter the water with an aquarium filter and provide an air stone to keep the water's oxygen level high. Feed the crayfish with worms or small feeder goldfish. Wrap black paper around three sides of the aquarium and place it away from direct sunlight. In order to keep the crayfish from crawling out of the aquarium, keep it covered.

Study the appearance of your crayfish and try to locate all of the external (outside) body features. Use the illustration on page 24 for comparison. Pay special attention to all of the appendages (extensions of the body). Notice that some appendages are used for sensing the environment (antennae) and some are used for eating. Others are used to bathe the gills with oxygenated water, and still others are used for crawling and swimming. Two swimmerets are used to aid in the mating process.

After observing the crayfish, answer the following questions in complete sentences.

1. What makes the chelipeds different from the other legs? ______________________________

____

____

2. How do crayfish use their tails to avoid being caught by you? ______________________________

____

____

3. Do you think your crayfish can actually see you? Why? ______________________________

____

____

4. Darken the aquarium as much as possible for a few minutes; then turn on a flashlight and describe any response by your crayfish.

____

____

5. Which appendages seem useful for eating? ______________________________

____

____

6. Is your crayfish a male or female? How can you tell? ______________________________

____

____

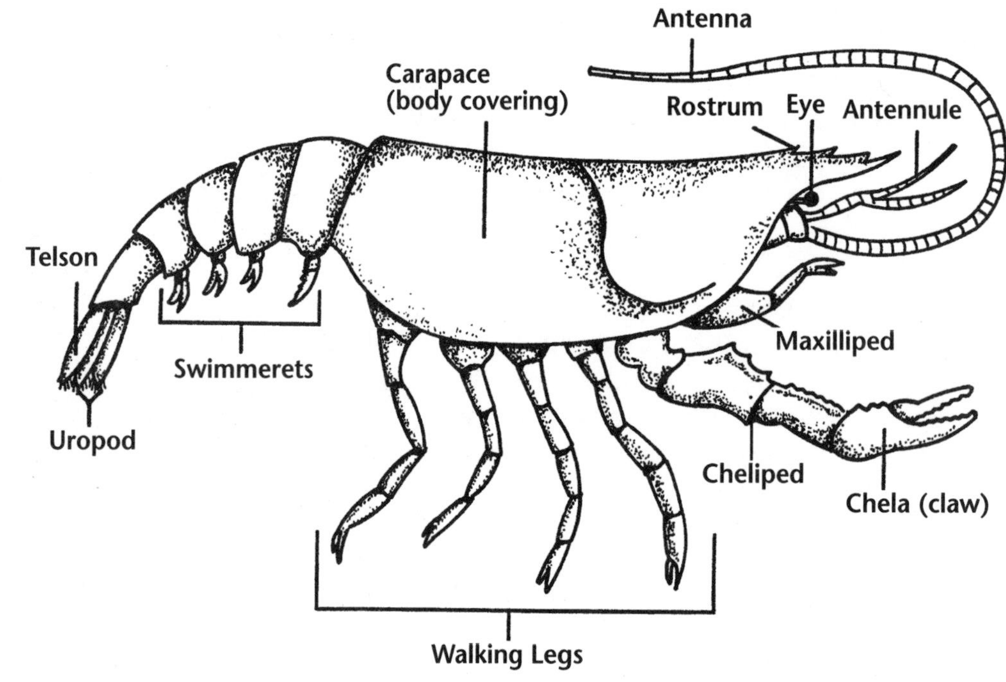

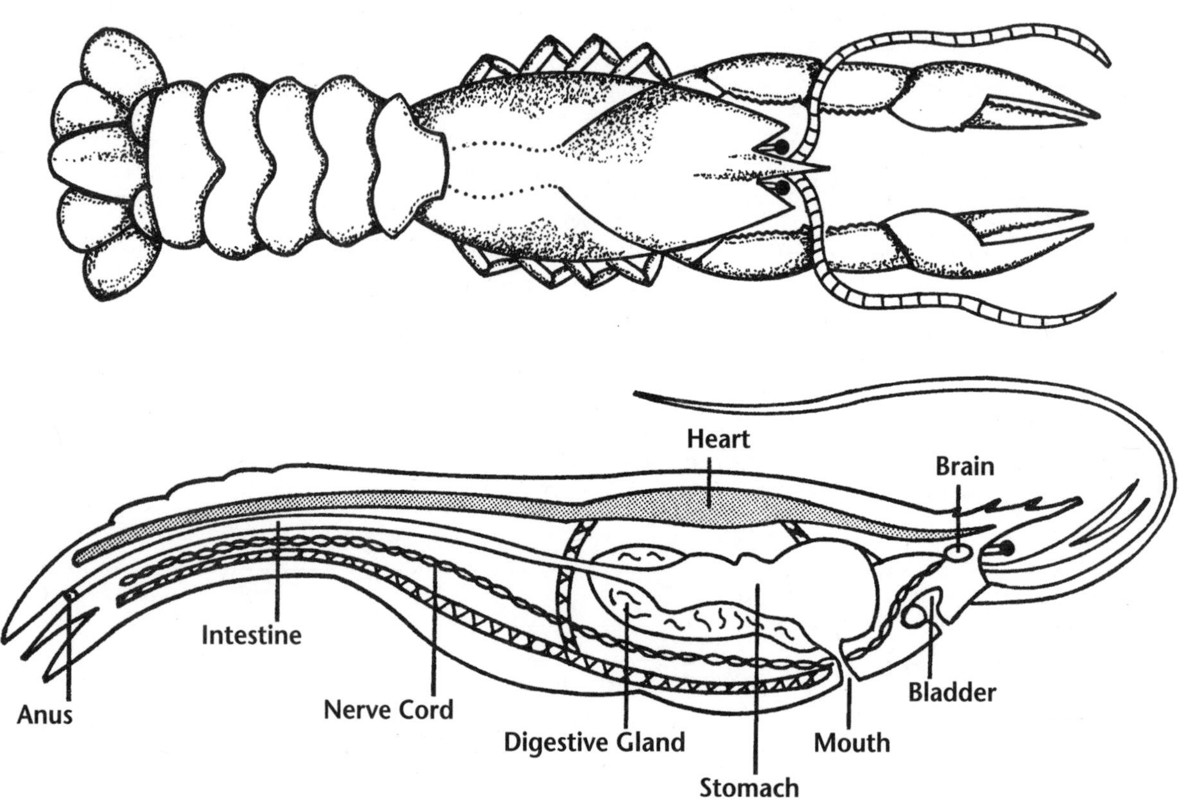

• Investigate—*Sow Bugs* •

Sow bugs are easy to find. Refer to page 22 to see what sow bugs look like and then search for them in moist areas under stones, logs, and leaves. Collect several bugs in a jar and add some damp soil and decaying leaves or grass (**humus**). Put a few air holes in the jar lid. Next, prepare a terrarium or large fishbowl by partially filling it with damp, rich humus. Include small rocks and partially decayed logs to serve as hiding places for these little isopods. Feed the sow bugs with an occasional thin slice of potato, apple, or lettuce leaf. Change these food items frequently so that they do not mold. Store the terrarium in a cool area.

Answer each of the following items.

1. Examine the shape of the sow bugs. Their shells are soft, flexible, and flattened. How might this compressed shape be useful to the sow bug?

   ____

   ____

2. What happens when you turn the sow bug over? How does the sow bug accomplish this motion?

   ____

   ____

3. Place a sow bug in a large test tube and place it in a refrigerator (not the freezer), for about an hour. What did the sow bug do? How might this body posture help it survive cold weather?

   ____

   ____

4. Place some sow bug droppings in a drop of water on a microscope slide and examine this under a compound microscope. What activity do you see?

   ____

   ____

5. Add a few sow bugs to a small sample of water for a few seconds. Gently swirl the water so as to bathe the entire creature. Remove the sow bugs and examine the water sample under a microscope. Draw a picture in the space below of any creatures found swimming in the water.

UNIT 2

Review

A Read the clues and write the correct word on the lines beside each number. Then follow the directions for the mystery word.

1. __ __ __ __ __ __ __ __ __ __
2. __ __ __ __ __
3. __ __ __ __ __ __
4. __ __ __ __
5. __ __ __ __ __ __ __ __ __ __ __
6. __ __ __ __
7. __ __ __ __ __ __ __ __
8. __ __ __ __ __ __ __ __ __
9. __ __ __ __ __
10. __ __ __ __ __ __ __

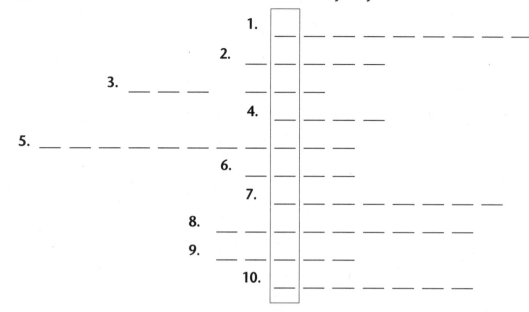

1. Crayfish have powerful claws at the ends of these limbs.
2. The opposite of salt water is ________ water.
3. One member of the wood lice family is the ________.
4. Some animals ________ in the water to capture prey while others wait, quiet and motionless, on the stream bottom.
5. The tough outer covering of arthropods.
6. Opposite of soft.
7. A smaller animal that resembles the lobster.
8. Gills are used for ________.
9. People with bad tempers are sometimes called ________.
10. This system helps animals sense their environment.

The **mystery word** is ________________________________.

B Name two other characteristics that all members of this animal group share.

1. ____
2. ____

Millipedes and Centipedes

Millipedes and centipedes both have long bodies and many legs. However, despite their similarities, these two kinds of arthropods are different enough to belong to separate groups. The term *millipede* means "thousand legs," and *centipede* means "hundred legs." As you will see, these names are somewhat misleading.

Millipedes

Millipedes are very common. They live in dark, damp places and usually feed on moist and decaying plants. Although some millipedes give off an **offensive** odor, they are harmless to humans and may be handled safely. They coil up their bodies **defensively** when handled. Millipedes are not insects, but they have insectlike heads. These heads include one pair of antennae and two clusters of **simple eyes.** Millipedes are plant eaters. They chew their food with their small mouths. The most striking feature of the millipede is its legs. All body segments, except for the first four, have two pairs of legs per segment. Although no millipede actually has a thousand legs, as the name suggests, some common varieties have 115 pairs of legs.

Centipedes

Centipedes are also very common. They live in many different kinds of environments. The kind of centipede you might find in a house is different than the kinds found in the forest and desert. As with the millipede, the most noticeable feature of a centipede is its legs. Unlike millipedes, centipedes have only one pair of legs per body segment. Some species have only fifteen pairs of legs while other varieties have over 170 pairs of legs. Some varieties are born with only seven pairs of legs. They gradually grow other legs after each molting.

Centipedes are active only in the dark. Compared to the slow-moving millipedes, they move rapidly. Once in motion, centipedes do not stop until their body is in contact with two sides of some object. Most centipedes are **carnivores.** They paralyze their prey with venom that comes from two specialized claws. Centipedes commonly eat soft-bodied insects such as cockroaches, plant lice, and silverfish. They will also eat snails, slugs, and earthworms. Although centipede bites are painful to humans, they are not generally harmful. Some varieties of centipedes reach about 30 centimeters (12 inches) in length.

Centipedes have one pair of antennae. The common house centipede has **compound eyes,** but other centipedes have simple eyes or no eyes at all. The centipede and millipede have similar internal structures for digestion, circulation, and breathing. Centipedes, like millipedes, reproduce by laying eggs. They have a flat body shape compared to the round, tubular shape of the millipede.

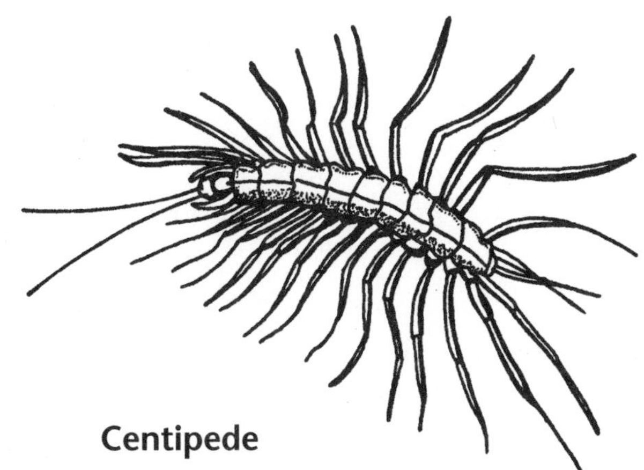

Centipede

UNIT 2

• Investigate—*Millipedes* •

Construct a terrarium according to the directions given on page 25. Collect several millipedes for your terrarium. Look under rotting logs, piles of moist leaves, and around foundation walls. The key to a successful millipede observation is to keep the environment moist but *not* soggy. If you are successful at raising millipedes, the female will lay her eggs in a nest made of earth. Notice how the female guards her nest. If the eggs hatch, observe how millipedes change during their growth and molting stages. During your observation, compare your millipedes with the illustration.

Millipede

After constructing the terrarium, observe the millipedes daily and become aware of their habits. Look for nest construction, feeding routines, and defensive and **offensive** (attack) behaviors towards other animals, including other millipedes. Remember to keep the environment moist. Store the terrarium in a dark area. Use the data table to document the activities of the millipedes. Date each entry.

Date	Millipede Diary

Review

Complete the following lists of similarities and differences between centipedes and millipedes. An example has been provided.

Millipede

1. No venom
2. __________
3. __________
4. __________
5. __________
6. __________
7. __________
8. __________

Centipede

1. Paralyzes prey with venom
2. __________
3. __________
4. __________
5. __________
6. __________
7. __________
8. __________

Insects

Something to Be Bugged About

Insects are the largest group of arthropods. There are more species of insects than of any other animal group. Scientists have identified about one million different kinds of insects, and thousands more are being discovered every year. The insects that are illustrated and discussed in this book represent a small sampling of orders, or groupings, of insects.

Insects are both harmful and helpful to humans. They create a major problem for farmers because insects destroy crops. Farmers fight their war against insects with chemicals (insecticides). Consumers pay higher prices for products at the supermarket because of the added expense of insecticide treatment. Insecticides may be harmful to humans, but there are not enough natural predators to control some insect populations naturally.

Some insects also cause damage to clothing, rugs, and furniture. They even eat the structural framework of houses. However, insects also perform many functions that are helpful to the earth. For example, insects are responsible for **pollinating** flowering plants. All field-grown plants need to be pollinated in order to produce seeds.

Each type of insect is only able to eat a certain kind of food. For example, some insects can eat only one plant species. Other insects may feed only on certain types of leaves or eat a rotting log only during one stage of decay. Because insects' diets are so specific, different insects do not compete with one another for food. Some insects are carnivores and eat other insects. Other insects are herbivores and eat plants. Many insects gather pollen and nectar for food. Some insects are parasites of plants or animals; others are scavengers. The type of food an insect eats determines its niche in nature.

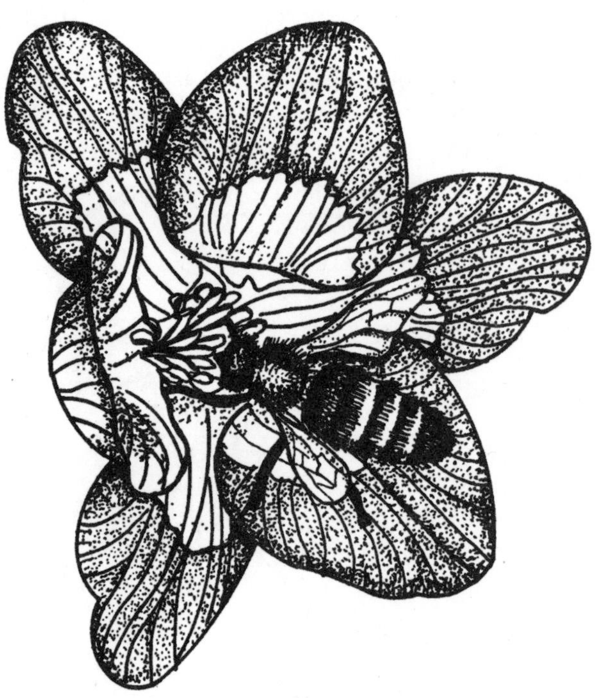

Bee Pollinating a Flower

Analyzing Insect Body Structures

All adult insects have the following three body sections: a head, a thorax, and an abdomen. The head contains the eyes, one pair of antennae, and the mouth parts. Most insects have a pair of compound eyes. They may also have three simple eyes. A compound eye has a series of lenses that gather the image from all directions at once. A simple eye structure has one fixed lens. The eyes of an insect never close.

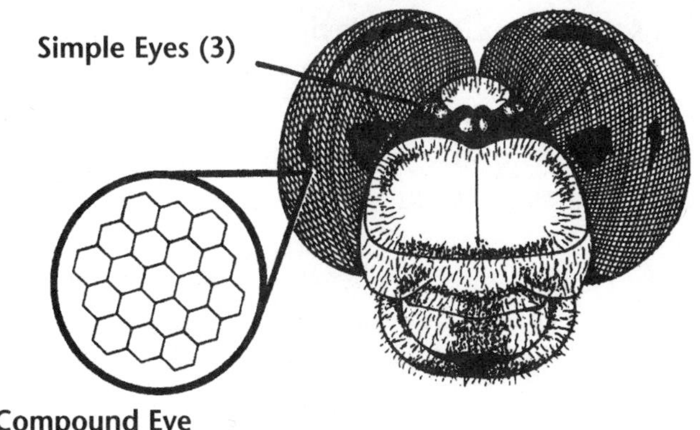

Insects use antennae to gain information about taste, touch, and smell. Some insects also use their antennae for hearing. There are several types of antennae.

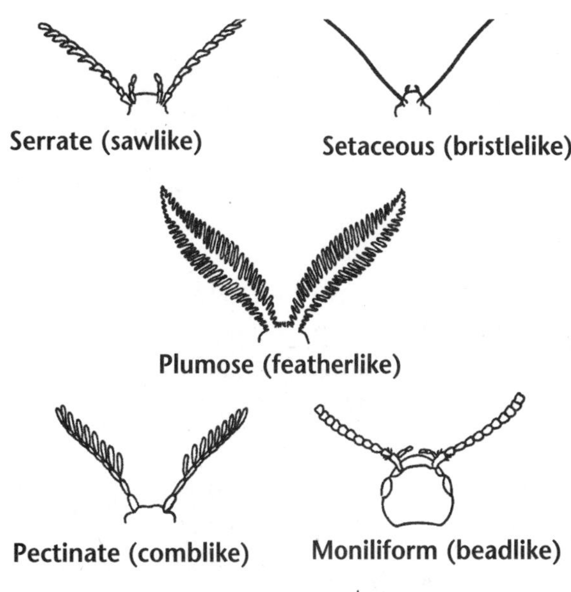

Insects' mouth parts are designed for different functions. Some insects have piercing and sucking mouths, some have only a sucking mouth structure, and still others have chewing or biting mouth parts.

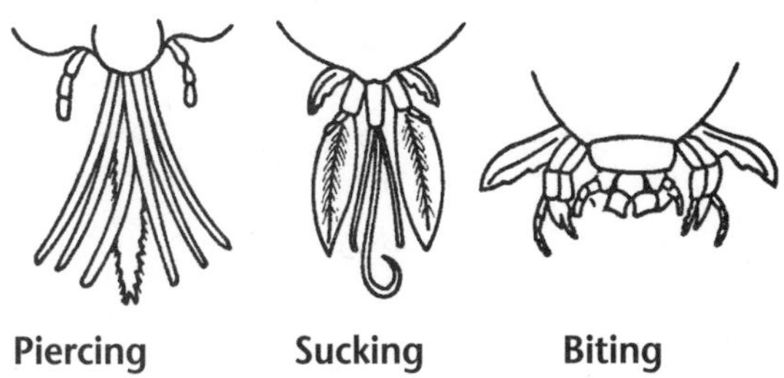

The thorax is the middle of the insect's body. It contains the muscles necessary to fly or walk. If the insect has wings, the thorax will contain two to four wings and possibly wing coverlets. A thorax always contains three pairs of legs. The leg structures of insect species vary. The structure of an insect's legs determine whether it can run, jump, catch, swim, hold, dig, or hang.

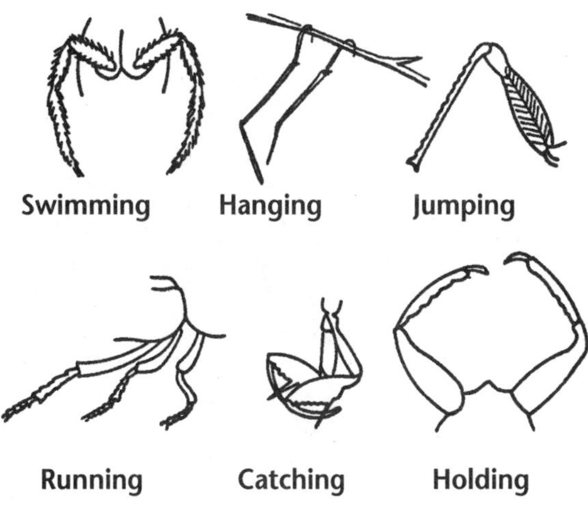

The third section of the insect body is the abdomen. This section contains the organs for digestion, reproduction, and breathing. The heart is also located in the abdomen.

Most insects reproduce by laying eggs. The adults usually leave the eggs and let them mature on their own. Some adult insects produce eggs only during one part of the year. Other insects release eggs on a continuous basis during the warmer months of the year. Many insects die during the winter and rely on the eggs that survived through the season to carry on the species.

When some insects hatch, they look like smaller versions of their parents. Other insects look nothing like their parents when they are born, and they change in form as they mature. This process is called **metamorphosis**, which means "changed form."

Complete metamorphosis consists of four stages: egg, larva, pupa, and adult. Insects in the *larval* stage often look like a caterpillar or a grub. As the insect matures and sheds its skin, it changes into a **pupa.** This is a resting stage. During this time the **cellular** structure of the insect changes to the adult form. When this process is complete, the pupa's casing (protective covering) splits and the adult insect emerges. This process takes only a few days for some insects and many months for other insects.

Some insects, such as the grasshopper, develop by **incomplete metamorphosis.** These insects go through three stages: egg, nymph, and adult. A **nymph** emerges from an egg and looks like an adult grasshopper. However, it is much smaller and its wings are not completely developed. After molting the exoskeleton several times, the nymph changes into a fully developed adult.

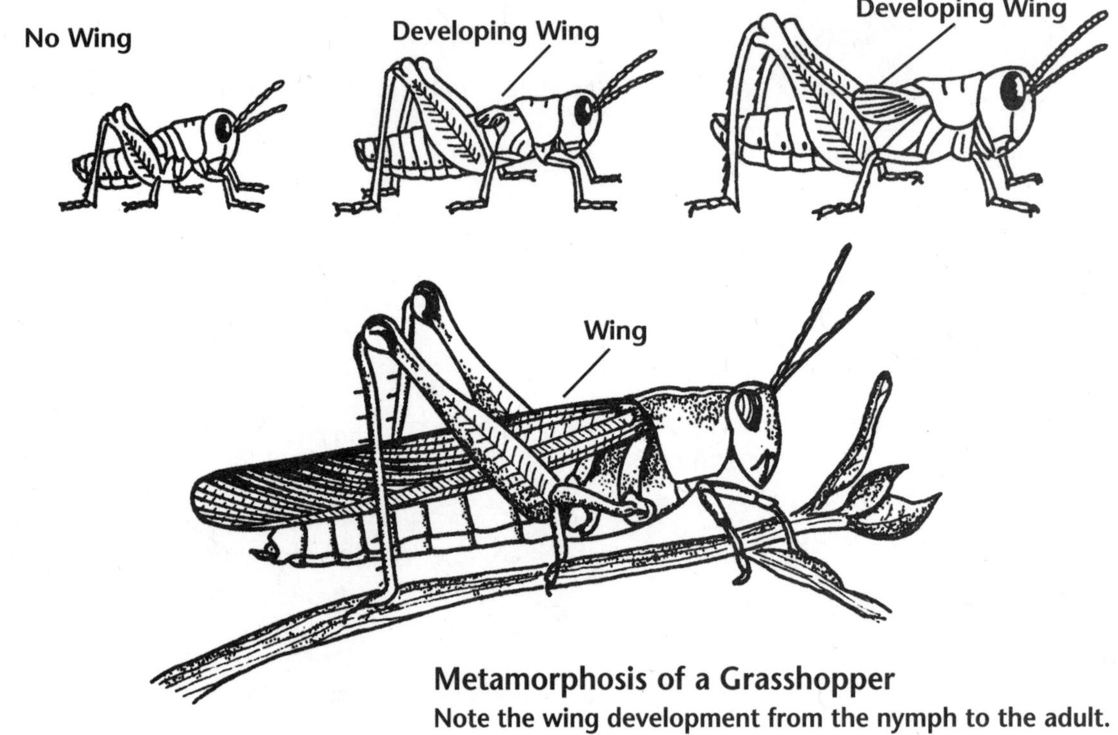

Metamorphosis of a Grasshopper
Note the wing development from the nymph to the adult.

Just as humans have internal structures to carry out body functions, so do insects. Adult insects breathe through the spiracles (tiny holes) along the sides of the abdomen. These openings allow air to pass through to the trachea (large tubes) that extend throughout the body of the insect. Oxygen is exchanged for carbon dioxide in each living cell of the insect's body.

Digestion is an important internal function in insects. The process is similar to digestion in earthworms because it is carried out without a true stomach. Food is passed from the mouth to the **gullet;** then it moves through the *crop,* **gizzard,** and, finally, the *intestine.*

All insects are poikilothermic (cold-blooded). This means that their body temperature varies with and closely matches the air temperature. Insects have many ways of dealing with heat and cold. They may warm themselves by working their wings together or cool themselves by avoiding the sun.

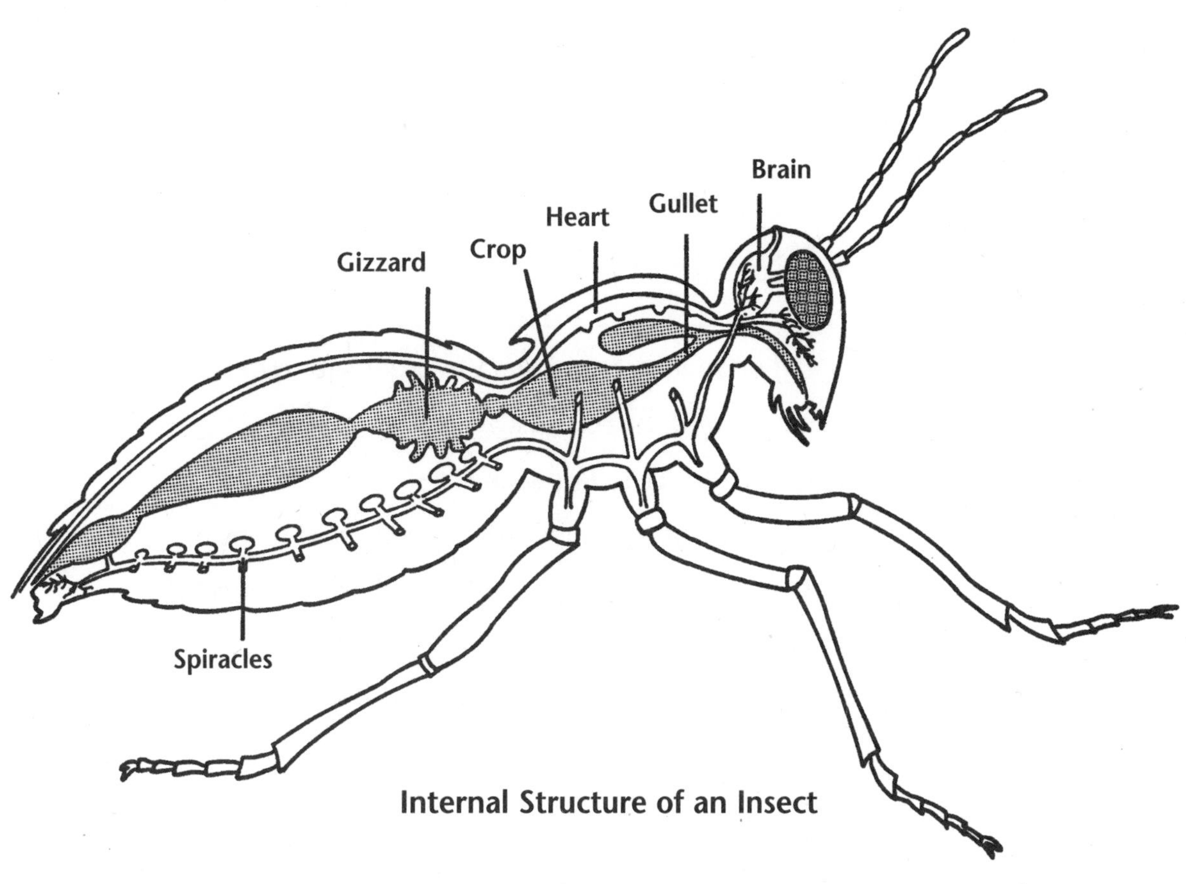

Internal Structure of an Insect

UNIT 2

Review

Choose the correct word from the word box and fill in the blanks of the paragraph. You may need to use a word more than once.

Word Box

simple	thorax
abdomen	larval
metamorphosis	stomachs
three	intestine
wings	spiracles
antennae	reproduce

Insects have **(1)**____________________ body sections. These sections are the head, thorax, and the **(2)**____________________. The head section has eyes, **(3)**____________________, and mouth parts. Compound and **(4)**____________________ eyes may both be present. The **(5)**____________________ is the section that contains muscles for flying or walking. An insect may have **(6)**____________________ to help it move. The **(7)**____________________ of an insect contains the organs for digestion, reproduction, breathing, and pumping blood. Insects **(8)**____________________ by laying eggs. The young of some insect species start in the **(9)**____________________ stage and change into a pupa. This series of changes from egg to adult is called **(10)**____________________. Insects breathe through pores called **(11)**____________________. Insects do not have true **(12)**____________________. They digest most of their food in their **(13)**____________________.

Beetles

The beetle is the most common type of insect. Some beetles create problems for humans. Many of them destroy plants and grain products. Others get into houses and eat carpets, draperies, and clothes. However, beetles are also helpful to people. Some beetles pollinate flowering plants that bees do not. Other beetles help control the population of harmful insects. The ladybug is one such beetle. This tiny hunter eats crop-destroying insects such as the harmful aphid, which sucks the sap out of tender plants. When aphids **infest** a plant, the plant eventually dies.

Beetles' bodies have adapted in many interesting ways. For example, fireflies, or lightning bugs, are soft-bodied beetles. They get their name from their ability to light up the tip of their abdomen. On summer nights, they blink their lights to attract a mate. This may be the only type of insect that uses sight to find a mate. Each species of firefly has its own distinctive flash pattern. One species has learned to duplicate the flashing cycles of other fireflies. When a male responds to this false mating signal, he is quickly seized and eaten by the imitator.

Beetles are different from other insects because they have a pair of special front wings. The leathery covers of these wings protect the beetle's body. Beetles come in a variety of body shapes and sizes. Some are so small that they can crawl through the eye of a needle. Others, huge by comparison, measure up to 15 centimeters (5 inches) in length. There are many beetle species. In fact, they represent 20 percent of all the living plant and animal species combined.

All beetles go through the four stages of complete metamorphosis. The egg matures on its own, and when it hatches it produces a larva, or grub. The grub molts several times. When it molts the last time it turns into a pupa. During this stage, the body begins to look like an adult beetle. After adult organs form, the pupa casing opens and an adult beetle emerges. The major activities of an adult beetle are to mate and reproduce.

■ Fill in the blanks with words or phrases from the text.

1. Many beetles are harmful because they eat ______________________________

   ____.
2. The ladybug beetle feeds upon the harmful ____________________.
3. Beetles also help ____________________ many plants that bees do not.
4. Fireflies attract each other by a series of ____________________.
5. A beetle develops in four stages through a process called ____________________.
6. The beetle egg hatches to form a ____________________, which changes first to a

   ____________________ and then to an adult.

UNIT 2

• Investigate–*Mealworms* •

In order to observe the developmental patterns of beetles, purchase a culture of mealworms from your local pet store. Separate the mealworms so that they are each in their own small container. Feed the mealworms oatmeal and an occasional thin slice of apple. The mealworms are in the larval stage of their development. Observe them as each changes from a larva into a pupa and then into an adult beetle. The metamorphosis should take about two weeks. Observe the mealworms' feeding habits and the shedding of the larval exoskeleton. If you miss the actual shedding process, look for the sloughed (discarded) exoskeleton. Keep a record of how many times the mealworm sheds.

Mealworm Data Table

Stage	What to Do	Date	Description
Larva	Describe the mealworms' length, eating habits, degree of activity, sensitivity to light, warmth, color, odor, and moisture. How many times was the skin shed?		
Pupa	Hold the pupa in your hand. Describe its movement and physical appearance. What body parts can you see developing?		
Adult	How long did this stage last? This beetle cannot hurt you. Pick it up and describe changes in color, appearance, and size. Describe how it responds to color, light, dark, warmth, and moisture.		

Butterflies and Moths

Many moths and butterflies are known for the impressive delicacy and color of their wings. Tiny scales on the surfaces of their wings are responsible for the variety of colors they exhibit. These scales rub off easily if handled. The wings will appear dull wherever they have been touched.

Butterflies and moths occupy different niches. This book will generally compare the two types of insects, but differences also exist among individual species of moths and butterflies. Moths tend to be active at night, and butterflies are more active by day. Moths often have feathery antennae, whereas butterfly antennae are stalklike and have knobs at the end.

Moths cause more harm to trees, shrubs, crops, and clothing than butterflies do. Moths and butterflies also hold their wings differently when they are at rest. Moths keep their wings outstretched and parallel to the ground. Butterflies close their wings above their backs.

Moths and butterflies also **pupate** differently. When the larva of a moth is about to pupate, it spins a silk cocoon to encase itself. Butterfly larvae attach themselves to a tree branch by a small bead of silk and hang upside down. While the larva is in this position, the exoskeleton splits open and exposes a new casing of toughened skin called a **chrysalis.**

Butterflies and moths also share some common characteristics. Both have two pairs of wings. One exception is that some female moths have no wings. Moths and butterflies undergo complete metamorphosis just as beetles do. Both use scent glands to attract mates, but butterflies are able to respond to species markings also. Compound eyes are a characteristic of adult butterflies and moths.

Complete Metamorphosis of a Moth

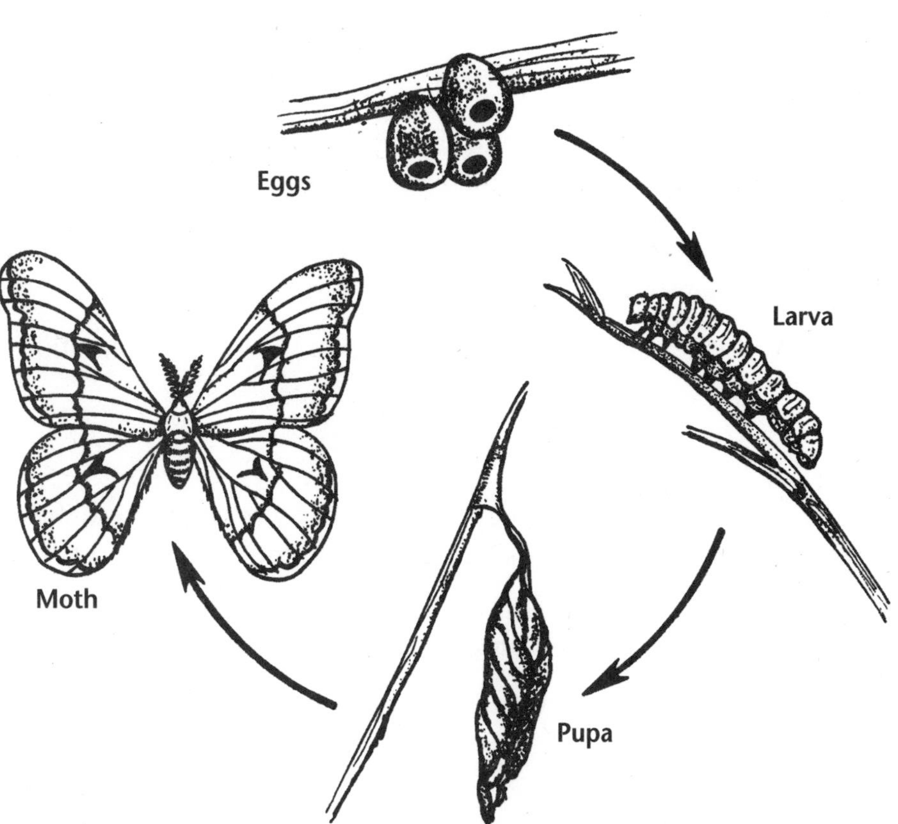

UNIT 2

• Investigate—*Butterflies* •

Raising butterflies provides you with an opportunity to observe their developmental stages up close. Butterfly kits can be ordered from a biological supply house for a moderate cost, or you can build an observation box on your own. Background research at the library will enhance the study.

Homemade Moth or Butterfly Observation Box

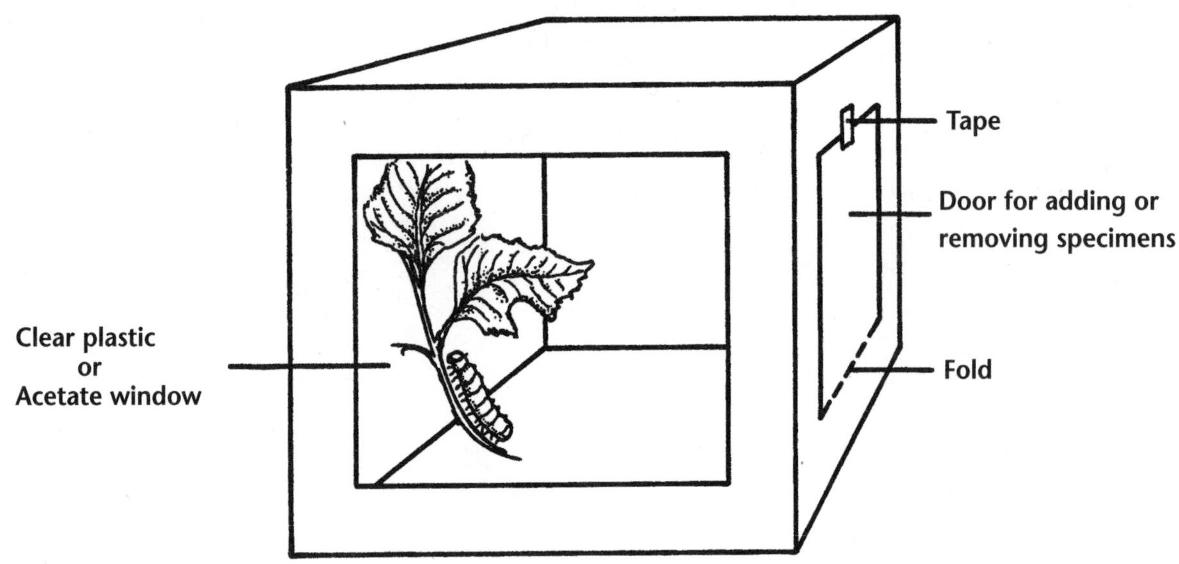

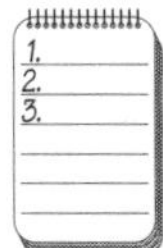

Procedure

1. Collect caterpillars and the food source that they depend on.
2. Place both the specimens and the food source in the box. (**Caution:** It is recommended that you wear gloves when handling unknown varieties of caterpillar because some have hairs on their bodies that cause a burning skin irritation.)
3. Observe the following, and write down your observations:
   a. feeding habits
   b. number of times skin is shed
   c. chrysalis or cocoon formation. Try taking close-up photographs. Glue a tag on the casing with the date metamorphosis was completed.
   d. days spent in pupation
4. Release your specimens after you have finished your observations.

Review

Fill in the chart with the phrases below. Some phrases may belong under both headings.

Moths	Butterflies

Active at night

Feathery antennae

Two pairs of wings

Compound eyes

Stalklike antennae

Active during the day

Larvae attach themselves to a branch by small bead of silk

Spins a silk cocoon

Scent glands

Wings outstretched when at rest

Wings upright when at rest

Ants

Social insects live in organized communities called **colonies.** The **inhabitants** of these colonies all have specific tasks to perform. Ants, bees, termites, and wasps are all examples of social insects. This book will discuss the social characteristics of these insects.

Ants

Every ant colony has at least one queen ant. The queen's responsibility is to lay eggs. Once in her lifetime, a queen ant goes on a mating flight with one or more male ants. Fertilization occurs during this flight, and the queen remains **fertilized** throughout her life. After she has been fertilized, the queen looks for a good place to build a nest. When she finds a proper location, she tears off her wings and digs into the earth. There she carves out a nursery in which she lays her eggs.

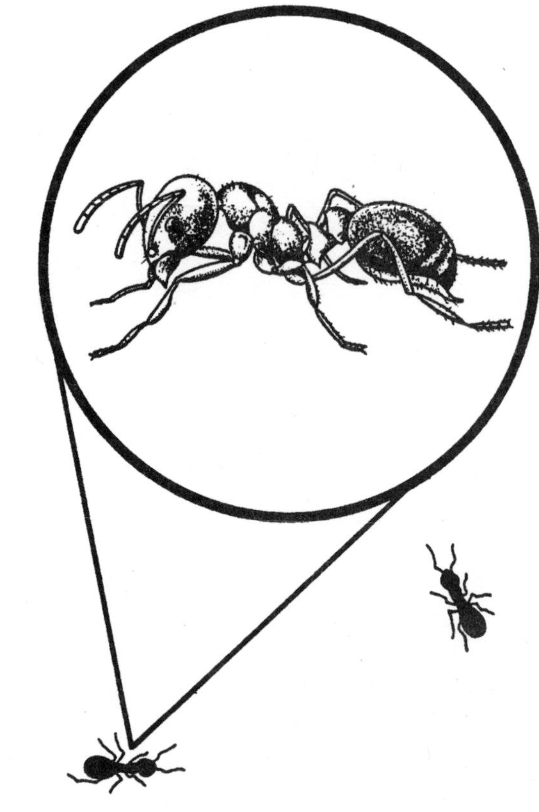

Larva emerge from the eggs and quickly enter into the pupa stage. As metamorphosis continues, the first ants to mature are female worker ants. They protect the nest and work to make the nest larger. They also take care of the queen. Later, male ants emerge. Their job is to fertilize new queens. When other queen ants develop in the colony, they usually leave with some of the male ants and form a new colony.

Different species of ants perform different tasks according to their needs. Some species, such as red and black field ants, raid other ant nests. They steal the larvae and make slaves of the developing ants.

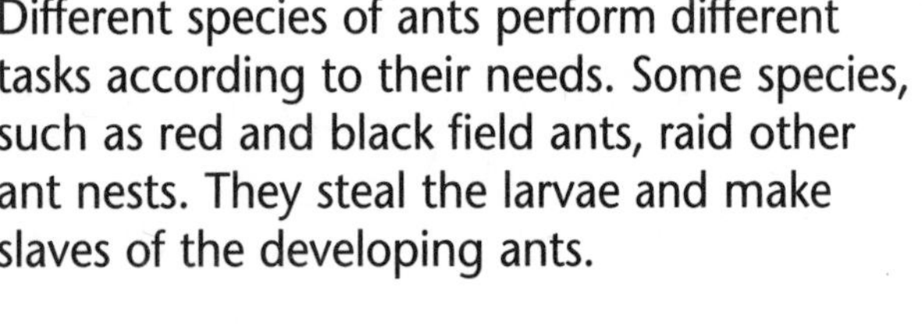

• Investigate—*Ant Farms* •

Ant behavior can be fascinating to study. You can order an ant kit from a biological supply house or you can dig up a wild ant nest and start a new colony. Your local library will contain books and reference materials that can help you learn more about ants.

Build Your Own Ant Farm

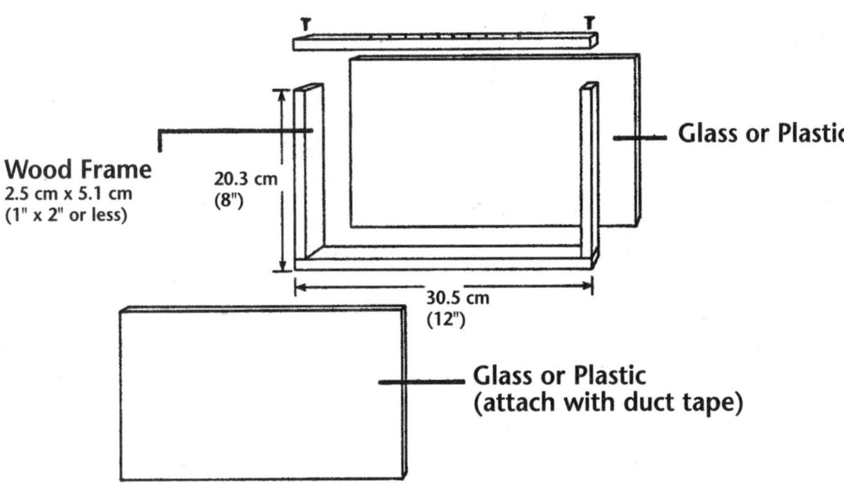

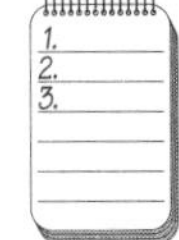

Procedure

1. Assemble your ant farm, leaving the top open.
2. Add moist sand or a mixture of sand and potting soil until the farm is about $\frac{2}{3}$ full.
3. Add ants to the farm and provide the ants with food. Food can include dead insects, tiny pieces of bread, and fresh leaves. Feed the ants about every two days.
4. Cover the top of the farm with a piece of fine screen or with a piece of nylon stocking.
5. Temporarily cover the outside of the glass with dark paper. This encourages the ants to construct the nest close to the glass, which will aid your observation.

 Circle "T" if the statement is true or "F" if the statement is false.

1. T F Ants live in colonies.
2. T F The queen ant's responsibility is to find food for the colony.
3. T F The queen ant tears off her wings and digs into the earth to lay her eggs.
4. T F The queen ant mates with the male in flight.

Bees

There are about 20,000 species of bees in the world. Bees are divided into two types: solitary bees and social bees. The most familiar example of the social bee is the European honeybee. There were probably no honeybees in North America until colonial settlers brought them over from Europe. The bees moved across the country, and when the pioneers moved westward, they found that the European honeybee had beaten them to the new territory. The honeybee is a valuable insect because it **pollinates** many plants.

Every bee colony, or hive, contains one queen, some drones, and many workers. Bees have a **rigid** social structure. Drones are male bees who fertilize the queen. Worker bees are all **infertile** females. They take care of the queen, build the **cells** in the hive, take care of the nursery, and gather pollen and nectar. Worker bees change their jobs many times during their short lives, and they work themselves to death. The workers live only six to eight weeks.

The queen bee has only one function, and that is to produce eggs. Once in her lifetime, the queen goes on a **nuptial flight.** During this flight she is fertilized by one or more drones and remains fertilized for her entire life. Queen bees develop when larvae are fed only **royal jelly** by the worker bees that take care of them. The first queen that emerges from the **brood** cells stings the other developing queens to death. The surviving queen must either leave the nest or kill or chase away the old queen. Queen bees live an average of three to five years.

In order to maintain their hives, bees need to communicate with each other. They do this by dancing. A worker bee who is scouting for food will return to the hive and do a dance. The direction of the dance, the speed of the dance, and the rate of speed at which the abdomen wags tell the other workers many things, such as the location, distance, and quality of a food source. Bee communication has been widely studied.

If you want to know more about bees, consider talking to a beekeeper. The state department of agriculture or a bee removal service will know of beekeepers in your area.

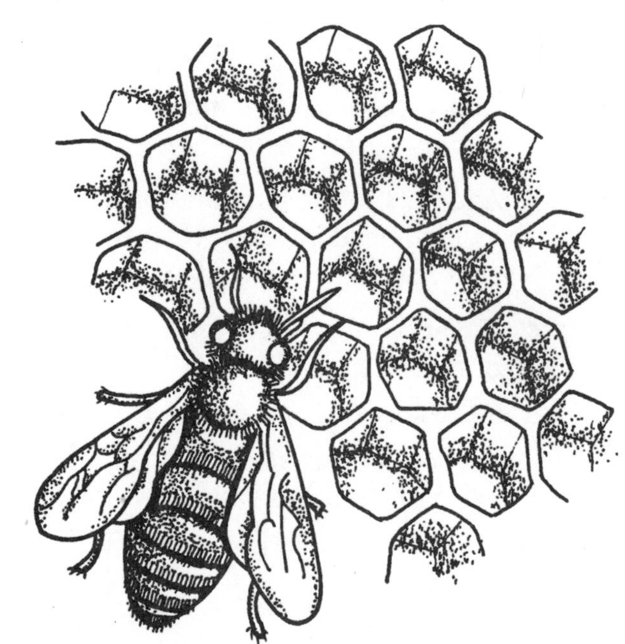

A Honeybee Worker on Honeycomb

Review

 Fill in each blank with the correct term or phrase. Choose your answer from the word box.

Word Box

dancing	caring for the nursery
fertilized	three to five years
honeybee	larvae are fed only royal jelly
location	six to eight weeks
lay	cell building
worker	caring for the queen

1. The ______________________ is a valuable insect because it pollinates plants.
2. During the nuptial flight, the queen bee becomes ______________________ for life.
3. New queens appear in the nest when ______________________________.
4. The queen bee's function is to ______________________ eggs.
5. The ______________________ bees gather pollen and honey.
6. Other jobs of the worker bee include ______________________________,

   ______________________________, and ______________________________.
7. Worker bees live ______________________________.
8. Bees communicate with each other by ______________________.
9. Queen bees live ______________________.
10. The distance, ______________________, and quality of a food source can all be communicated by dancing.

UNIT 2

Termites

Termites are sometimes called white ants, but this is an inaccurate name. Termites have more in common with cockroaches and grasshoppers than they do with ants. There are over 40 species of subterranean (underground) termites in the United States. Because termites destroy wood, they are often considered pests, but they perform a beneficial service in nature. A termite's niche is to **break down** dead trees and shrubs and return the nutrients back to the soil so that they can be used by living plants. Termites do not actually digest the wood they eat. **Bacteria** or protozoa in their digestive tract break down the wood **cellulose** into a nutritious form that they can use.

Most termite colonies have three groups of inhabitants: workers, soldiers, and royal males and females. The majority of termites in the nest are workers. They take care of the royal members, feed and groom the soldiers, maintain and expand the nest, and search for food. Workers may be either male or female.

Soldier termites are highly specialized members of the nest. These creatures have enlarged heads and oversized mandibles (jaws). They use their mandibles to defend the nest against the termites' major enemy, the ants. The soldiers are unable to feed themselves because of their mandibles, so in many termite species workers feed and groom the soldiers.

Only the royal male and female termites reproduce. Some of their offspring are new **reproductives** who leave the nest and fly a short distance to begin a new colony. The male and female remove their wings and establish a permanent residence when a site has been selected. The success of the nest depends upon the availability of food, the ability of the termites to defend the nest against predators, and the nest's ability to survive natural disasters such as fire or flooding.

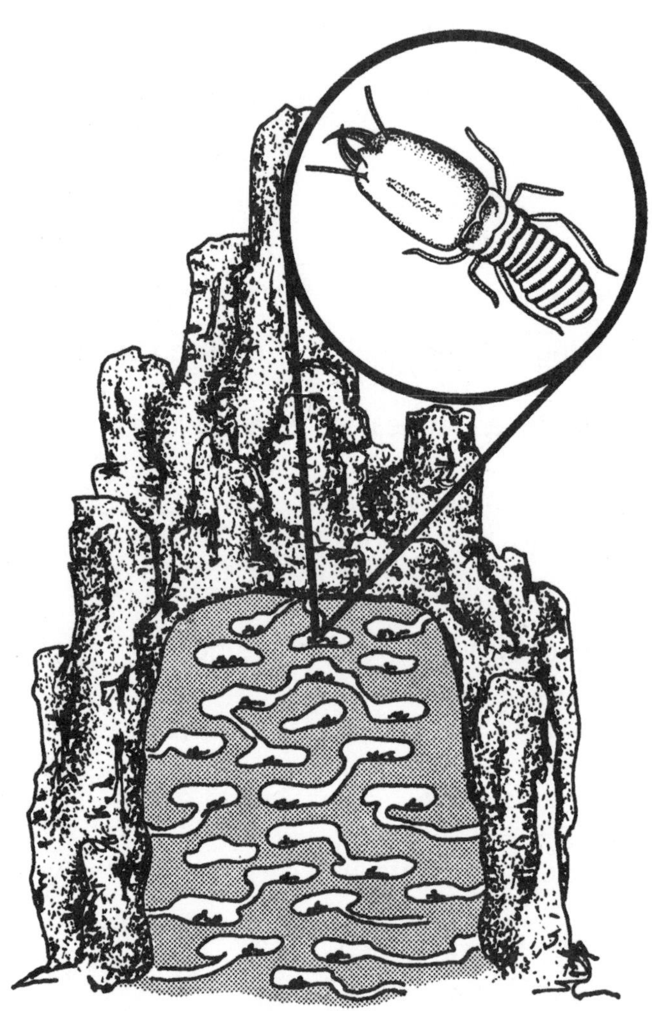

Termite Nest and Close-up of Soldier Termite

Review

UNIT 2

 Fill in the blanks using the words from the word box.

Word Box

reproduce	soldier
cockroaches	bacteria
colony	wings
grasshoppers	breaking down
workers	underground
ants	

1. Termites are closely related to ______________________ and ______________________.

2. Subterranean termites live ______________________.

3. Most of the termites in a nest would be classified as ______________________.

4. Some termites depend upon ______________________ in their digestive tract to break down wood so that they can get nutrients from it.

5. Termites with enlarged heads and mandibles are the ______________________ termites, which defend the nest.

6. Major enemies of termites are ______________________.

7. The only termites that ______________________ are the royal males and females.

8. New reproductives fly a short distance to begin a new ______________________.

9. Reproductives remove their ______________________ when a nest site is selected.

10. Termites help nature by ______________________ dead trees and shrubs.

Wasps

Like bees, wasps may be divided into two groups: solitary wasps and social wasps. Social wasps have a system of labor similar to that of ants and bees. There is usually one queen to a nest that includes many female workers. The only function of the males is to mate with the queen.

Most social wasps produce one of two types of paper nests. Some species produce a small comb-shaped nest out of paper. The comb is made of one layer of many six-sided cells. These nests are often found under eaves and soffits (roof overhangs) of buildings. Other species make a ball- or pear-shaped nest that contains multiple layers of cells. These nests have a single entrance and may be found in trees and bushes or on the ground in abandoned rodent holes. Yellow jackets are one kind of wasp whose ground-level nests have painfully surprised people as they mow their lawns.

The Chinese, who were the first people to make paper, report that they learned the skill by watching wasps. Queen wasps are the ones who build nests. A queen spends the winter in a cocoon, and when she emerges she selects a spot on which to build. She makes the paper for the nest by chewing soft wood and leaves. The queen lays an egg in each cell after the nest is finished.

The eggs mature and hatch out as larvae. For about two weeks, the queen feeds this first brood bits of insects that she has hunted and chewed. The larvae spin cocoons around themselves, and while encased, they become pupas, similar to moths. An adult worker wasp comes out of the cocoon. The queen continues to lay eggs while the workers take care of the nest and the queen's needs.

Each wasp species has a particular niche in nature. Although most adult wasps eat mainly flower pollen, these daytime hunters prey upon many types of insects and spiders in order to feed their young. Wasps, although bothersome to humans, help control the population of many insect species.

Wasp and Comb-Shaped Nest

Review

Circle the "T" if the statement is true and "F" if the statement is false.

1. T F There are usually three queens in a wasp nest.
2. T F Wasps enter their nests from the top.
3. T F The yellow jacket is a kind of wasp.
4. T F The wasps go through larval and pupal stages before becoming adults.
5. T F Wasps are of no value to humans.

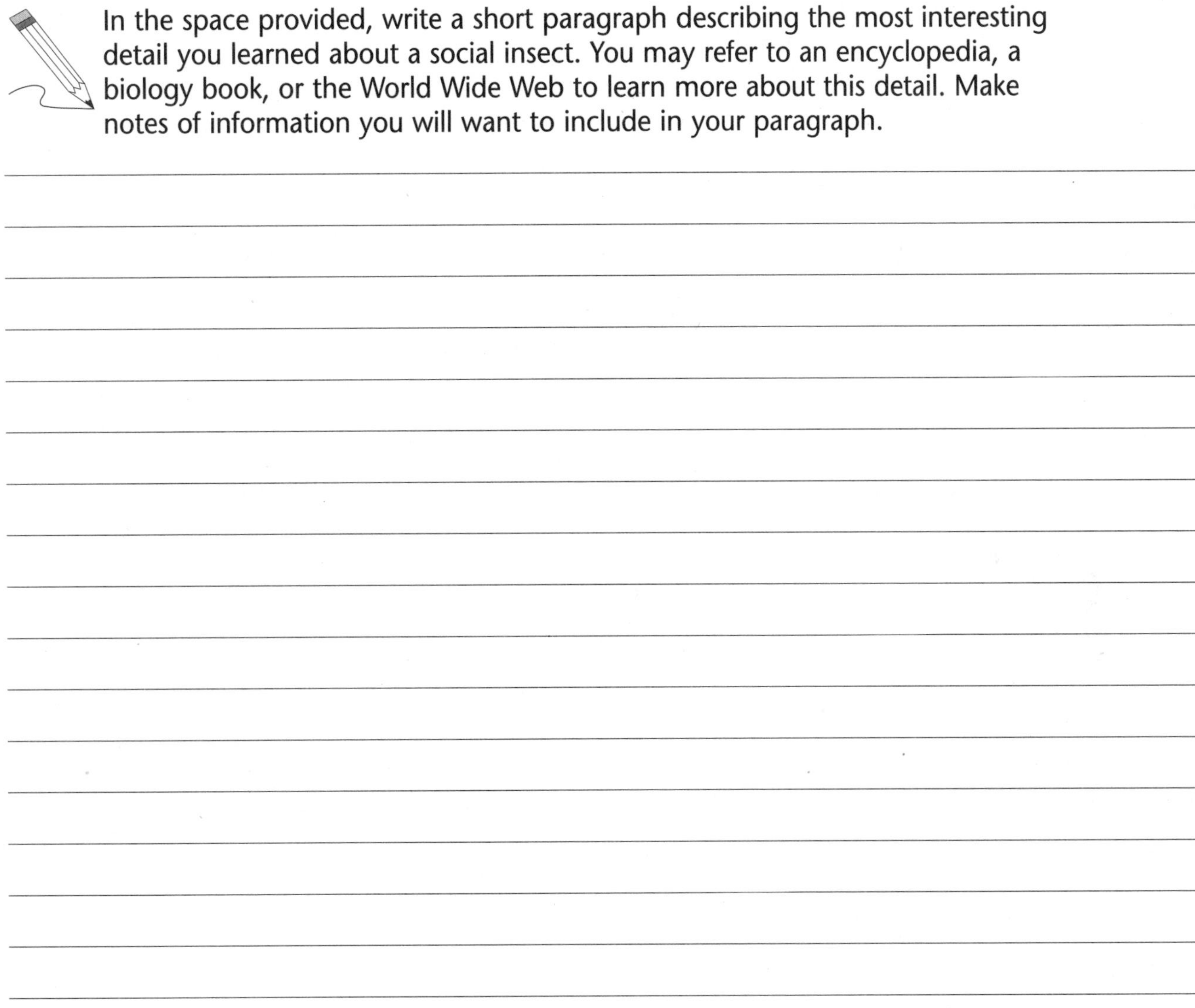

In the space provided, write a short paragraph describing the most interesting detail you learned about a social insect. You may refer to an encyclopedia, a biology book, or the World Wide Web to learn more about this detail. Make notes of information you will want to include in your paragraph.

R E V I E W

Review Unit 2

A Match the words in Column A with the best word or phrase from Column B. Write the letter by the words on the line.

Column A	Column B
______ 1. break down wood cellulose	a. gather pollen and nectar
______ 2. worker bees	b. queen bees
______ 3. paper nests	c. colonies
______ 4. subterranean	d. microscopic organisms
______ 5. social insect communities	e. underground
______ 6. live 3 to 5 years	f. wasp
______ 7. white ants	g. social wasps
______ 8. high degree of intelligence in the insect world	h. termites

B Answer the following questions in complete sentences.

1. In what ways are mites different from spiders? ______________________________

____

____

2. Compare the ways scorpions reproduce with reproduction in spiders, mites, and ticks.

____

____

3. Explain why crustaceans are important to fish. ______________________________

____

____

4. Why do most crustaceans have bristles extending from various parts of their exoskeletons?

____

____

5. What survival processes do most crustaceans exhibit when they lose an eye or a leg?

____

____

C Circle the letter of the best answer.

1. Queen ants and queen bees are alike in that ______.
   a. they are the same size
   b. they both sting
   c. they are fed pollen
   d. after mating, they remain fertilized their entire life
2. Termites are useful insects because ______.
   a. they destroy houses and furniture, thus keeping these two industries busy
   b. they break down soil
   c. they break down dead trees and shrubs
   d. they loosen soil and improve drainage
3. Queen wasps build their nests by ______.
   a. burrowing through dead wood
   b. turning wood and leaves into paper
   c. collecting pollen to make honey
   d. swarming around a branch or hole
4. European honey bees ______.
   a. flew across the Atlantic and populated North America
   b. are known for their killer instinct
   c. were brought to America by settlers
   d. make paper
5. Another name for termites is _____.
   a. flying ants
   b. white roaches
   c. white ants
   d. wood ants

D Fill in the blanks with the best word or phrase from the text.

1. The word "millipede" suggests that this animal has ____________________ legs.
2. Millipedes may be found in areas containing ____________________.
3. Millipedes eat ____________________.
4. A millipede has ____________________ ____________________ of legs attached to most of its segments.
5. Millipedes have ____________________ eyes.
6. The small mouth of the millipede is designed for ____________________.
7. Some millipedes defend themselves by ______________________________.
8. Unlike millipedes, centipedes get their food by ____________________.

UNIT 3

Chordates

Cosmopolitan and Specialized

Scientists organize and describe **life forms** according to **traits** that make them different from one another. Animals in the chordate group are structured very differently than other animals. Chordates are cosmopolitan, which means they are found all over the world. They occupy every environment on earth, but most of them are aquatic (live in water). Members of the chordate group vary greatly in appearance. As you will see, both some unusual animals and some very common ones belong to this group.

The following features characterize members of the chordate group:

- a tubular nerve cord—a hollow cord that is a major part of a central nervous system.
- a notochord—simple support structure for the nerve cord. A vertebral column replaces the notochord in more complex animals.
- gill slits—these disappear early in the developmental stages of land animals; they later become the bony structure of the middle ear.

All chordates have the features described above during at least one stage of their development. For example, although gill slits are not found in mature human beings, they are present during the **embryonic** stage.

The most advanced chordates are **vertebrates,** the group that has an internal skeleton and a vertebral column made of **cartilage** or bone. Vertebrates include animals of all sizes, from tiny mice to large whales. This book will discuss amphibians, reptiles, birds, and mammals, and will provide a quick reference to some of the unique features of each of these animal classes. Each group contains many thousands of species that will not be discussed here, and readers are encouraged to conduct further research on their own.

Whale

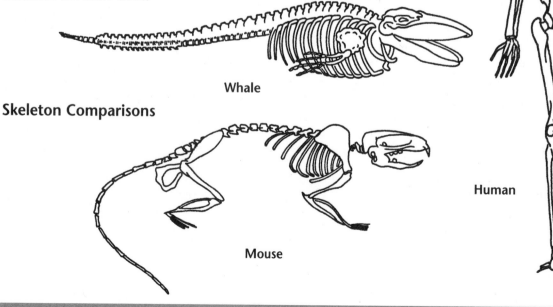

Skeleton Comparisons

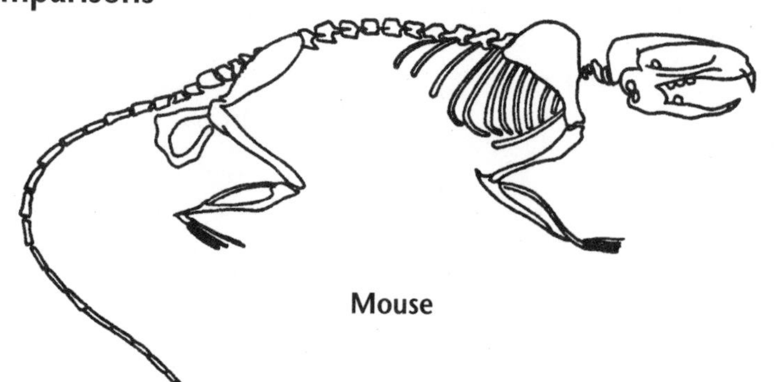

Mouse

Human

UNIT 3

Review

Answer the following questions in complete sentences.

1. What animals have a tubular nerve cord and gill slits at some point in their lives?

____

____

2. What happens to the gill slits when land animals reach full maturity?

____

____

3. How do scientists assign animals to different groups?

____

____

4. What is the most advanced group of chordates called?

____

____

5. Next to each of the following animals write "yes" in the blank if they are vertebrates and "no" if they are not vertebrates.

birds ______________

reptiles ______________

insects ______________

mammals ______________

amphibians ______________

spiders ______________

earthworms ______________

crabs ______________

Amphibians

A Different Approach

The name *amphibian* comes from a Greek word meaning "living on both sides." "Both sides" refers to land and water. Amphibians are animals that have moved onto the land but are still dependent upon water for part of their life cycle. In North America, two animal types belong to this unusual group: (1) frogs and toads and (2) salamanders.

Some of these creatures must keep moist because they breathe through their skin much like earthworms do. Other members of this group breathe by means of gills. Some amphibians rely almost entirely upon lungs.

Although some amphibians give birth to live young, most frogs, toads, and salamanders reproduce by releasing eggs in freshwater. In a few cases, the eggs are **incubated** in moist earth or the moist, rotting debris of a log. The eggs hatch into larvae, which change into adults through metamorphosis.

When the egg casings break, larvae with gills are released. These larvae have flattened tails and tiny limbs or no limbs at all. The larvae of frogs and toads are called tadpoles. The tadpole stage is similar to the larval stage of insects. It may last a few weeks to a few years, depending upon the species. The young tadpole eats **algae.** It eventually becomes a carnivore. In some species, the tadpole eats its own brothers and sisters.

As the frog or toad larva develops, its tail shortens and its hind legs begin to show. The front legs eventually appear and the mouth widens. At this point, toads (and some frogs) leave their watery environment and don't return until they are able to reproduce. Reproduction is the one factor that keeps these creatures bound to an aquatic environment.

Amphibians are poikilothermic (cold-blooded). This means that their body temperature changes with the air temperature. Amphibians that live in cold climates burrow themselves into the soft earth and **hibernate** to survive the winter months. During this period of sleep, their heart rate slows down to four beats per minute. They do not eat when they are hibernating.

Salamanders

Salamanders are different from other amphibians because the adults possess a tail. For this reason, many people confuse salamanders with lizards. Salamanders differ from lizards in that they have no scales, claws, or external ear openings. Their legs stand out from their body farther than those of a lizard. Despite their tails, salamanders are more similar to frogs and toads than they are to lizards.

Salamanders are *carnivorous* and eat worms, grubs, insects, amphibian eggs, and sometimes other amphibians. Except for reproductive purposes, most salamanders live on land. They are often found in forests under rocks and logs.

There are over 370 species of salamanders in the world, and many of them live in North America. Some species no longer go through the full metamorphic process. They skip the larval stage, which means that the salamander hatches out of the egg as a creature that looks like a miniature adult.

Some salamanders raised in **captivity** can live more than twenty years. The largest salamander in the United States, the hellbender, may reach a length of 90 centimeters (3 feet). However, most salamanders are only a few inches or centimeters long and are safe to handle. These creatures are not *venomous.* Only a few varieties are likely to bite a human.

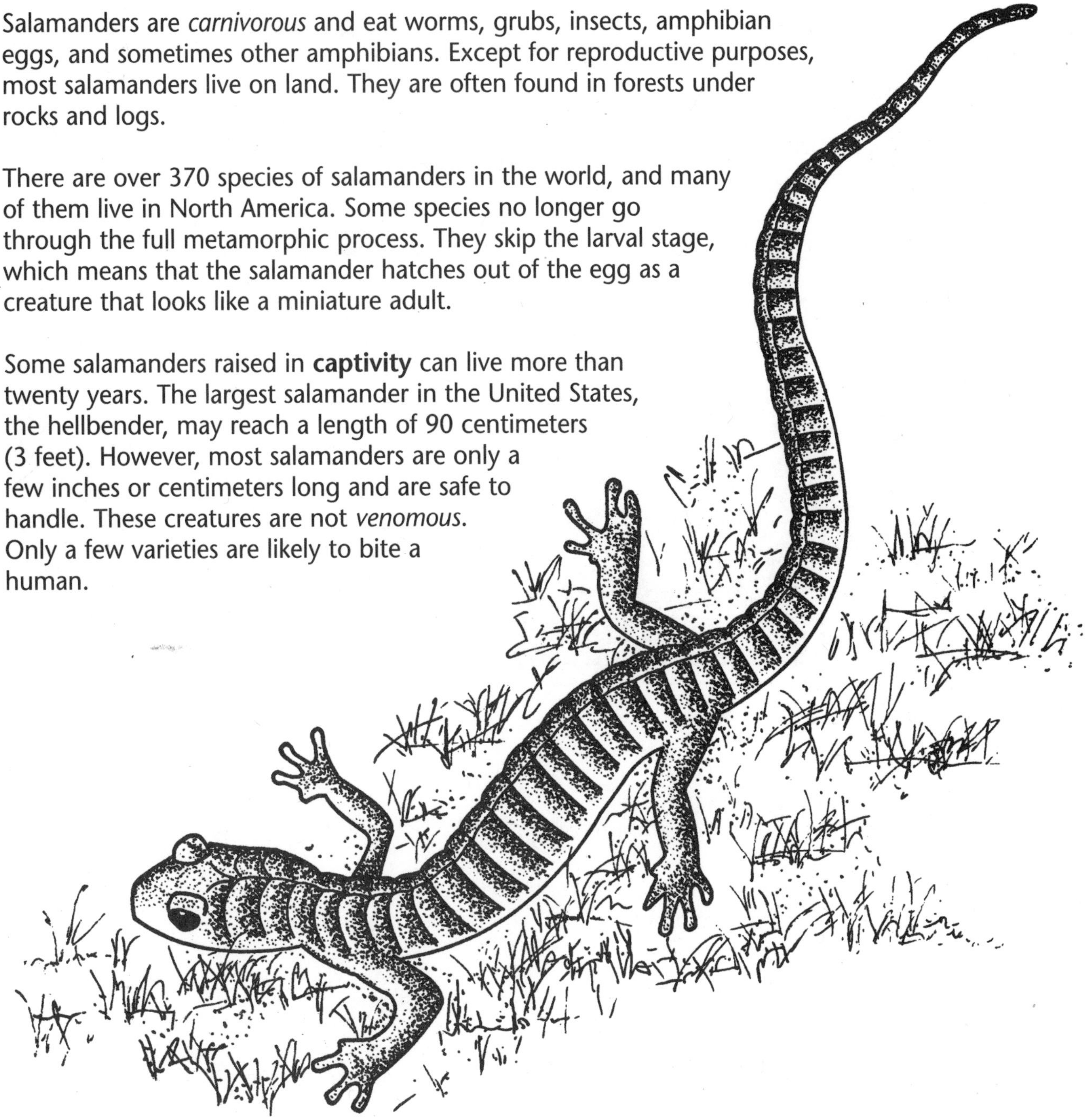

UNIT 3

• Investigate—Constructing a Terrarium •

Salamanders are fun to watch. Look for them under rocks and trees in wooded areas and then follow the directions below to set up a terrarium that is similar to their natural environment. Return your salamander to its natural environment after a week or so.

Terrariums can be of any size and need not be elaborate. A large jar can make an attractive and functional environment for plant and animal study. Be careful not to crowd too many plants in a terrarium. The terrarium needs light, but not direct sunlight. Direct sunlight will overheat your terrarium.

Large terrariums can be made by having pieces of glass cut to size. Tape or caulk all edges to make a sturdy, watertight seal. Duct tape can be used to seal the edges. The following illustration shows a commercially made terrarium.

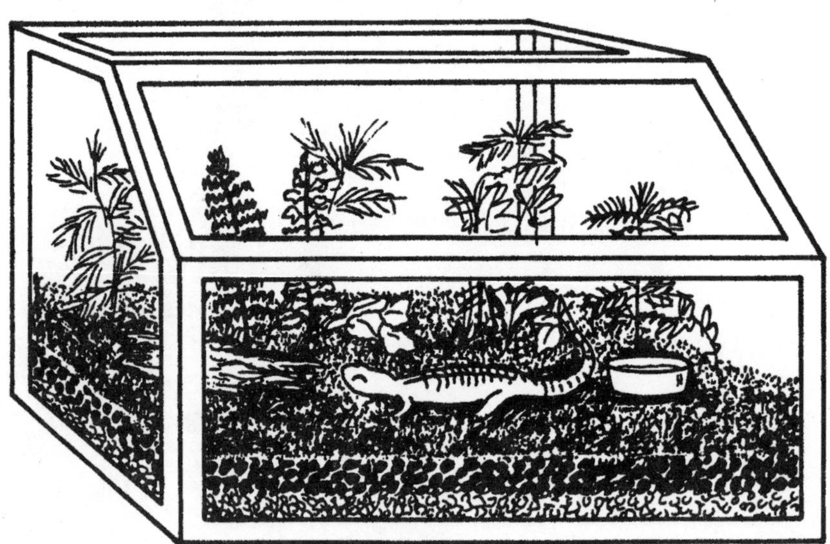

Procedure

1. Cover the bottom of your terrarium with gravel. This will help provide drainage.
2. Add a layer of aquarium charcoal to reduce decay odors.
3. Carefully add $2\frac{1}{2}$ to 4 centimeters (1 to $1\frac{1}{2}$ inches) of potting soil or garden soil mixed with sand.
4. Add wild plants or store-bought ones.
5. Dampen the soil.

Optional: Add insects, salamanders, worms, spiders, a rotting log, millipedes, or a water dish.

Maintain a record of the health of organisms in your terrarium. Describe any changes that occur such as changes in color, the death of certain organisms, flowering, new growth, fungus growth, and any adjustments that were necessary on your part to maintain life in your terrarium.

Terrarium Log	
Date	**Description**

Frogs and Toads

Frogs and toads are the largest group of amphibians. These two kinds of animals are very closely related. They both have bulbous bodies, no tails, and a good sense of hearing. Male frogs and toads make noise to attract mates. The females lay their eggs in still, shallow water. Frogs and toads both are extremely adaptable and can live in cold and damp, as well as hot and dry, climates.

The animals do have some differences. The dry and bumpy skin of true toads is different from the smooth, slick skin of frogs. Behind the toad's eyes are two large bumps called warts. The warts release a fluid that bothers predators. The giant toad, found in the southern part of the United States, releases a **toxic substance** that can kill a dog if it attempts to pick up the toad in its mouth. Humans can handle these creatures safely but should wash their hands thoroughly to avoid getting the toxin (poison) into their eyes. Toads have shorter, less powerful legs than frogs. Unlike frogs, they do not have teeth in their upper jaw. Otherwise, frogs and toads are almost identical in their body structure.

Both frogs and toads are very helpful to humans because they eat many insect pests. Toads are often found around the foundations of houses. They can find their prey easily in these areas because many insects are attracted to the warmth and moisture that collects there.

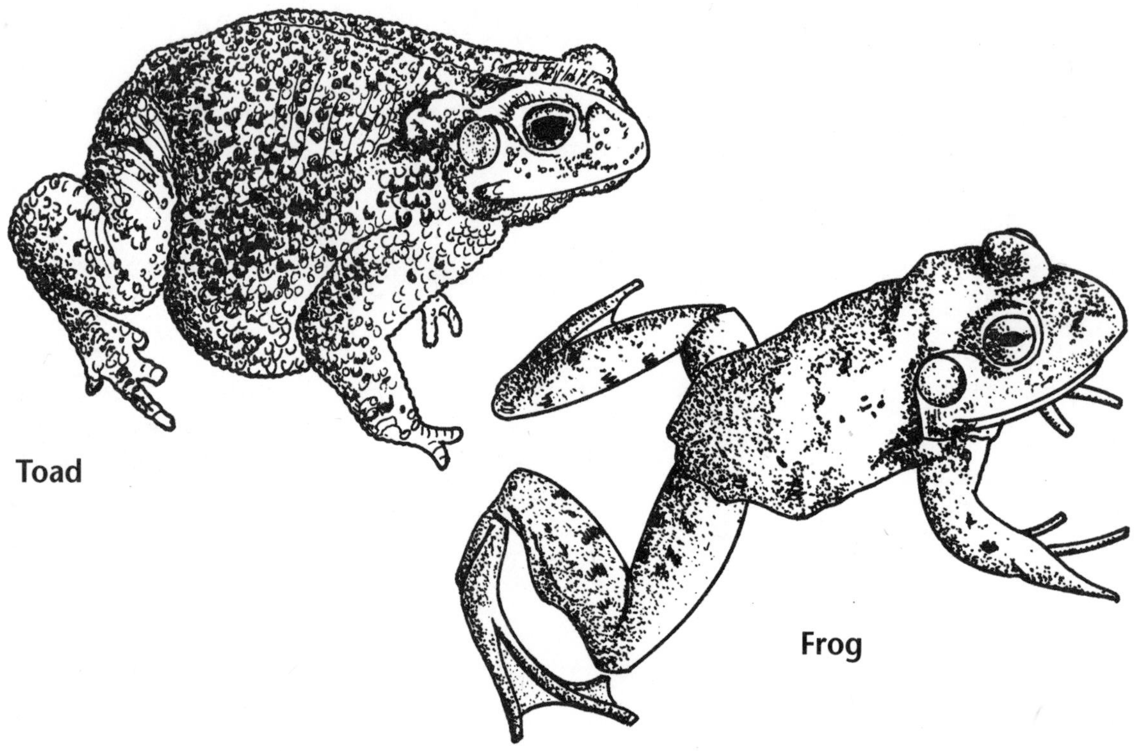

UNIT 3

Review

Answer the following questions using complete sentences.

1. What does the name amphibian mean? ______

2. Name two kinds of amphibians.

3. What metamorphosis does a frog go through? ______

4. Can an amphibian live in a desert environment successfully? ______

5. Do amphibians have a constant body temperature? ______
   Explain. ______

6. What do salamanders eat? ______

7. Are salamanders dangerous? ______

8. Remember that a salamander is an amphibian.
   How do salamanders that live in cold climates survive the winter? ______

9. How are frogs and toads helpful to humans? ______

10. Where are toads often found? Why? ______

11. Tell one way in which frogs and toads are different. ______

12. Tell one way in which frogs and toads are similar. ______

• Investigate—*Frogs and Toads* •

Most frogs and toads undergo metamorphosis. This gradual process can be observed in an aquarium. In the spring, collect an egg mass from a pond or slow-moving stream. Also collect a few gallons of the water in which you found the eggs, and use that to fill the aquarium about halfway. (Do not use tap water that has been treated with chlorine and fluorine.) Use an air stone and an aquarium pump to keep the water full of oxygen. Put a few rocks from the stream in the water and gently add the eggs. Tadpoles will hatch in a matter of days. In the meantime, watch the embryos develop by placing a few eggs in a petri dish and observing them under a **stereomicroscope.**

Once the tadpoles hatch, rapid growth will take place if there is a rich supply of algae. Change the aquarium water frequently by adding fresh pond or stream water. Many frog species complete the process of metamorphosis in six to eight weeks. Make a note of changes during this period. Provide a place for the developing frogs to climb out of the water, or else they will tire of swimming and drown. Return the frogs to their native stream and allow them to finish their life cycle under natural conditions.

Record observations two times each week.

Tadpole Observation Log		
Week	**Date**	**Observation**
Week #1		
Week #2		
Week #3		
Week #4		
Week #5		
Week #6		
Week #7		

Reptiles

A Legacy of Success

Reptiles have been on the earth for a very long time. During the Mesozoic Period of the earth's history, which started about 240 million years ago and ended about 65 million years ago, reptiles called dinosaurs ruled the earth. In fact, the Mesozoic Period is sometimes called the Age of Reptiles. The remains of land animals are not usually preserved as well as those of marine (sea) animals, but the dinosaurs from this time left a remarkable fossil record.

Fossil skeletons have provided scientists with information on the feeding habits, environment, and size of these early reptiles. Although many people think that all dinosaurs were very large, the fossil evidence reveals that the average-sized dinosaur was approximately 130 centimeters (4 feet) tall. However, giant dinosaurs did exist. Many natural history museums around the country have exciting dinosaur exhibits.

Scientists compare the bone structure of dinosaurs with reptiles of today by studying fossil skeletons. New ideas about the dinosaurs' relationships to modern animals develop as research on prehistoric animals continues.

Diplodocus

Modern Reptiles

Although some crocodiles and snakes are over 6 meters (20 feet) long, most modern reptiles are relatively small in size. Reptiles are poikilothermic (cold-blooded). These vertebrates have scaly skin and breathe with lungs. There are four groups of reptiles: the turtles, the snakes, the lizards, and the crocodilians.

Unlike amphibians, reptiles have adapted to laying their eggs on land. Most reptile eggs have a tough outer **membrane** that prevents the eggs from drying out. Since they do not have to live or reproduce in water, reptiles can move about the land, exploring various environments. In the last 200 million years, land masses have moved, and the world's climate has changed many times. Most reptiles have gradually adapted to these changes and so are very different from their early ancestors. However, reptiles continue to thrive in most parts of the world. The United States, with its mild climate, is home to members of each of the reptile groups represented in this book.

Complete each sentence with words or phrases found in the text.

1. Fossil skeletons provide scientists with ______________________________

____

____

2. The average-sized dinosaur was ______________________________

____

3. The Mesozoic Period started about ____________ years ago and ended about ____________ years ago.

4. List three characteristics of reptiles: ______________________________

____

____

____

5. Describe a reptile egg: ______________________________

____

____

Turtles

Fossil evidence shows that turtles have been on the earth for over 200 million years. Their body design has changed very little in that time. Turtles have a spinal cord and a vertebral column that run along the middle of the shell. Bony plates spread out from the spine. These plates are actually flattened ribs that have almost fused together. They make up the inner layer of the shell. The turtle also has a hard outer shell that is permanently attached.

Turtles have survived events that have caused the mass **extinction** of other species. Apparently, something about their physical makeup and habits has **ensured** their survival. However, many turtles today are in danger of extinction. This is primarily because humans have destroyed many turtles' habitats. Although a turtle's shell protects it from most natural hazards, it offers no protection against automobiles and power lawn mowers. At present, there are about 50 species of turtles in North America north of Mexico.

Different turtles have different habits, depending on where they live. However, all turtles share some basic traits. For example, all turtles lay their eggs on land. The eggs have a leathery shell, and the turtles that hatch from them all have soft shells for the first few years of their lives. Some turtles, such as the box turtle, may hatch as the weather starts to get cooler. When this happens, they burrow immediately into the soft soil and decaying plant material and hibernate through the winter months.

After the female turtle lays her eggs, she does not return. Turtles are on their own as soon as they hatch. Scientists have wondered how young turtles know what is safe to eat. The answer seems to lie in a process called chemical imprinting, in which the mother's feeding habits are passed on to the egg by means of **chemical compounds.** Although many young turtles are killed by predators, turtles have a long life span. Turtles in captivity often live beyond 40 years. The common box turtle may live longer than 100 years.

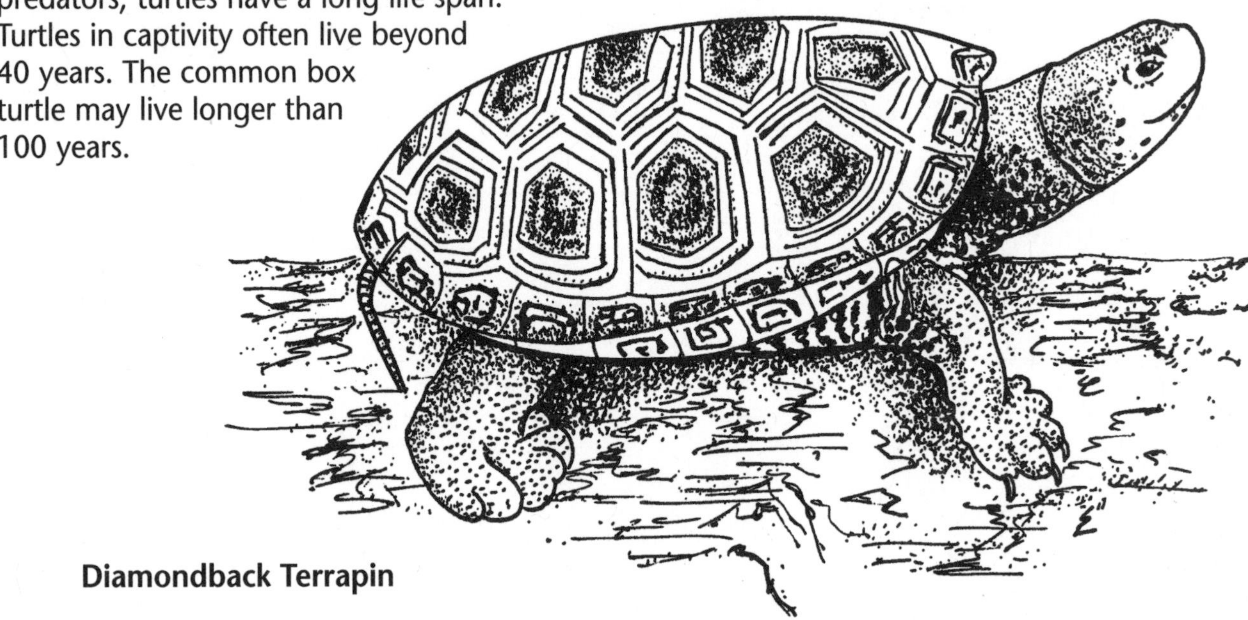

Diamondback Terrapin

Turtles grow fast during the first few years of life. This growth slows down as the turtle becomes an adult. The shell expands as the turtle grows. When some turtles grow, a ring appears on the scutes (plates) that cover the back of the shell. It has been suggested that counting the rings will reveal a turtle's age. However, the rings eventually become crowded and worn and are useless as a means of measuring a turtle's age.

Snapping turtles and musk turtles are known to bite, but other turtles are safe to handle. When studying turtles, keep them in captivity for only a short time. Always return the turtle to the place where it was found. Take pictures and make detailed drawings to study at greater length. This way, you will not interfere with the turtle's **instinctive** behavior.

 Underline the correct answer.

1. Turtles have gone through (many, few, no) body changes over the years.
2. Turtles have a (muscle, organ, spinal cord) that runs along the middle of the shell.
3. Turtles have (fangs, shells, poisonous venom) as a protection against predators.
4. The most serious threat to turtles is (habitat destruction, predators, disease).
5. During the winter months, turtles (migrate, die, burrow).
6. Turtles have (spines, growth rings, holes) on the plates of their shell.
7. Young turtles may know what to eat because of (chemical imprinting, habit, copying).

Snakes

Snakes have flexible, limbless bodies and predatory habits, which makes many people dislike them. However, snakes are fascinating creatures. They have a unique body structure because all of their internal organs have been stretched to accommodate their long, slender shape. In addition, most snakes have only one lung.

The eating habits of a snake are also unique. A snake can open its mouth wide enough to swallow prey that is larger than the **diameter** of the snake's head. Snakes do not chew their food and so must swallow their prey whole. Each side of the jaw moves independently and directs the prey down the throat. All snakes have teeth that they use to prick their prey and keep it from escaping. As the prey moves into the stomach, the ribs and various connective tissue spread out to accommodate the food.

Since snakes have no limbs, they use their mouths to capture their prey. Some snakes, such as the garter snake, begin to swallow their prey as soon as they strike it. Constrictor snakes, like the black rat snake, seize their prey by biting it and then quickly coiling their body around the animal. Every time the captured animal exhales, the snake tightens its grip until the animal suffocates.

Other snakes capture their prey with venom. A snake's venom is a deadly **neurotoxin.** A neurotoxin paralyzes the prey to make it easier for the snake to handle. This reduces the chance that the snake will be injured by its prey during the attack. Even so, studies show that some snakes have been attacked by their victims. Most snakes wait until their prey has died before they swallow it.

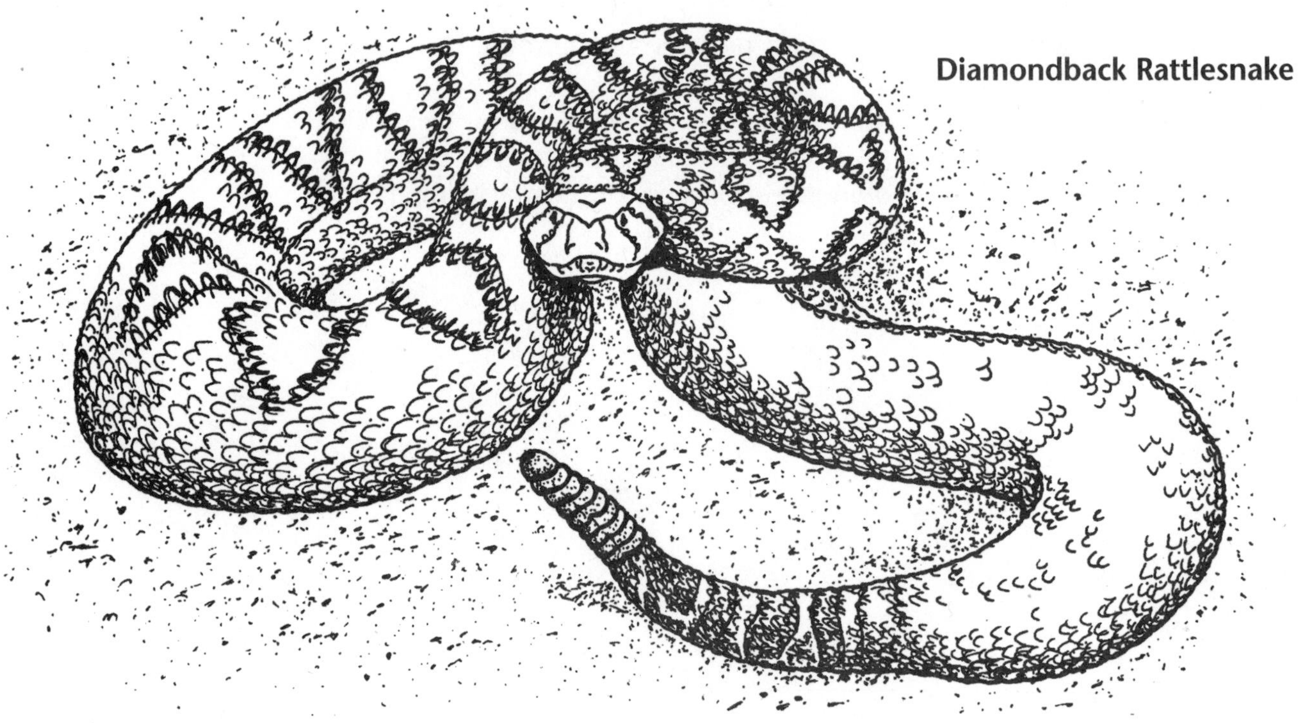

Diamondback Rattlesnake

There are 136 species of snakes in North America. Copperheads, cottonmouths, rattlesnakes, and coral snakes are some examples of venomous snakes found in the United States. The bites from these snakes are painful and may be fatal to humans, but proper treatment can prevent death. Coral snake bites are particularly dangerous. However, coral snakes have a small mouth and short fangs. This offers humans some protection, since clothing, boots, and garden gloves will usually keep the fangs from penetrating the skin. Coral snakes are related to the cobras, a group of poisonous snakes that live in Africa, Australia, and Asia.

Snakes eat birds, lizards, fish, frogs, and rodents, among other things. This diet determines their niche in nature. They help control the rodent population. They also help control the snake population, since some snakes eat other snakes. For example, the king snake has been known to devour venomous snakes such as rattlesnakes, copperheads, and coral snakes.

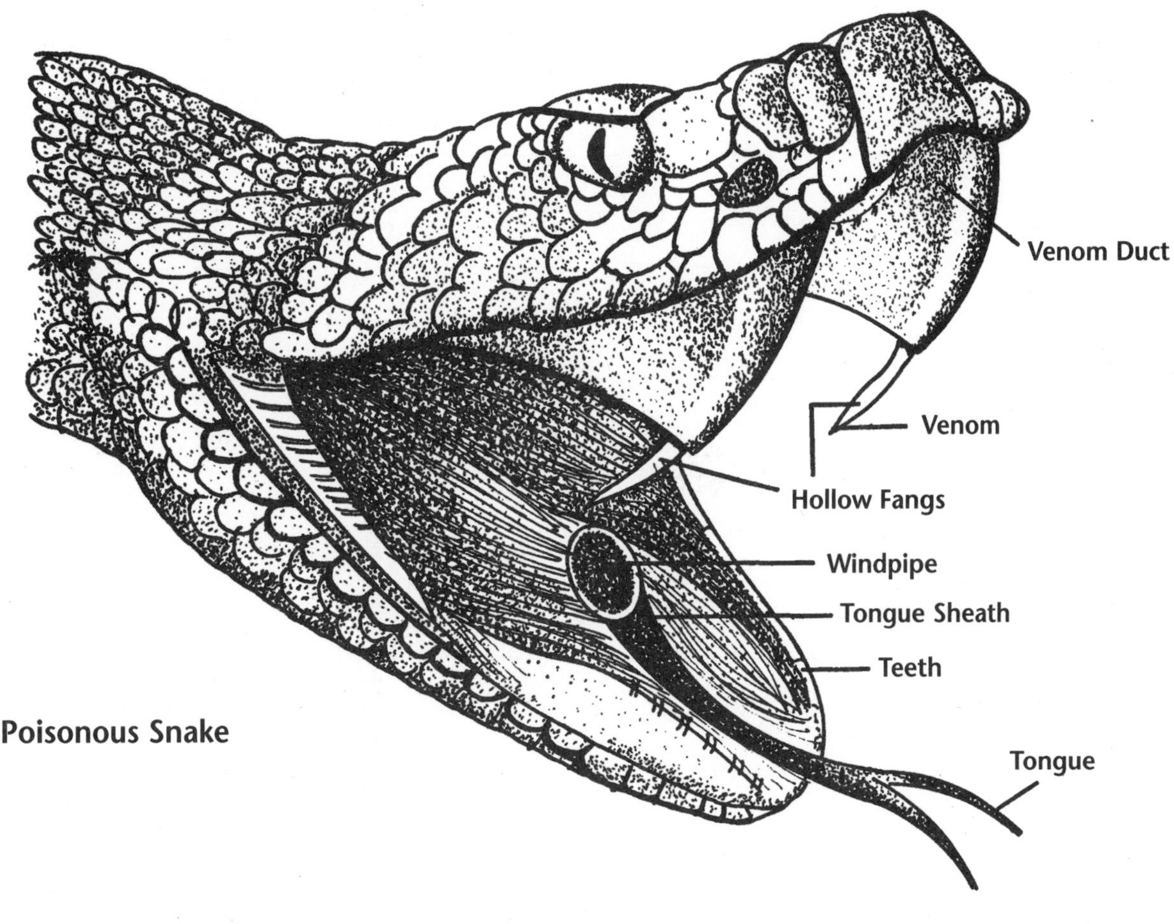

Poisonous Snake

UNIT 3

• Investigate—*Snakes* •

After reading some additional information on snakes, construct a poster that will help educate the public about the positive characteristics of these animals. Make your poster clear and attractive, and consider using humor to get your point across. **Suggestion:** Invite a specialist in herpetology (the study of reptiles and amphibians) to speak to your class. You may be able to contact a herpetologist through a zoo.

Find sentences from this lesson that contain the words in the list. Write the complete sentence in which each word is found.

1. diameter______________________________

2. jaw ______________________________

3. constrictor ______________________________

4. venom ______________________________

5. paralyzes ______________________________

6. rodent______________________________

7. exhales ______________________________

8. species ______________________________

9. neurotoxin______________________________

Lizards

Lizards are remarkably similar to their ancestors of Mesozoic times. They exist in a large range of sizes. Some geckos are only $2\frac{1}{2}$ centimeters (1 inch) long, while the Komodo dragons of Japan grow to about 3 meters (10 feet) in length. There are 115 species found in the United States. Most North American species are relatively small, but the common iguana can reach nearly 2 meters (6 feet) in length.

These creatures fill a variety of niches. Some are herbivores and eat plants, but most are carnivores and eat meat, including insects that are bothersome to humans. The majority of North American lizards are diurnal (active during the day). A few lizards are nocturnal (active at night). Only two North American lizards are venomous, the beaded lizard of Mexico and the Gila monster of the American southwest.

Lizards are seen most frequently in the warmer areas of North America and are harder to find farther north. In order to find these creature in the wild, learn about their habits and search out the type of environment in which they can be found.

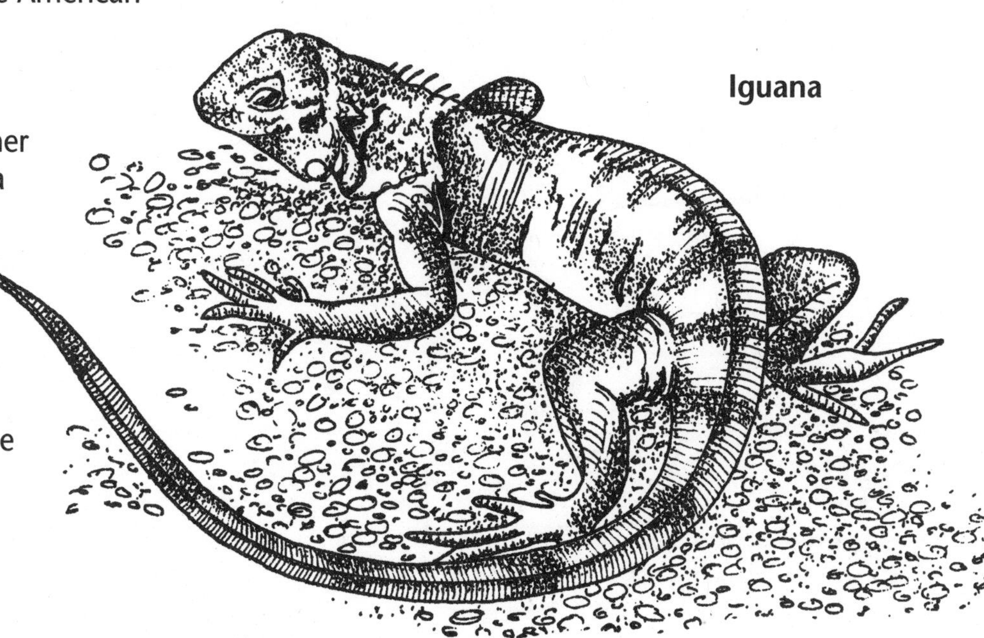

Iguana

Find the words in the section above that have the following meanings. Write the words in the space provided.

1. Active at night ______________________
2. Meat eater ______________________
3. Active during the day ______________________
4. Plant eater ______________________

Crocodilians

Crocodilians have been on earth for over 200 million years. They lived through the extinction of the dinosaurs, some 65 million years ago. Some of the ancient crocodilians reached a length of almost 15 meters (about 50 feet)! Although no crocodilian living today is that big, crocodilians are the largest of living reptiles.

Crocodilians are aquatic animals that live in warm waters. They are different from other reptiles in that they have a four-chambered heart like that of birds and mammals. Their diaphragm is almost complete. It separates the chest cavity from the abdominal cavity.

There are only two species of crocodilians that are native to the United States: the American alligator and the American crocodile. The map below shows where these species can be found. Each of the American species reproduces by laying eggs in a mound of decaying vegetation. The decaying process releases heat which incubates the eggs.

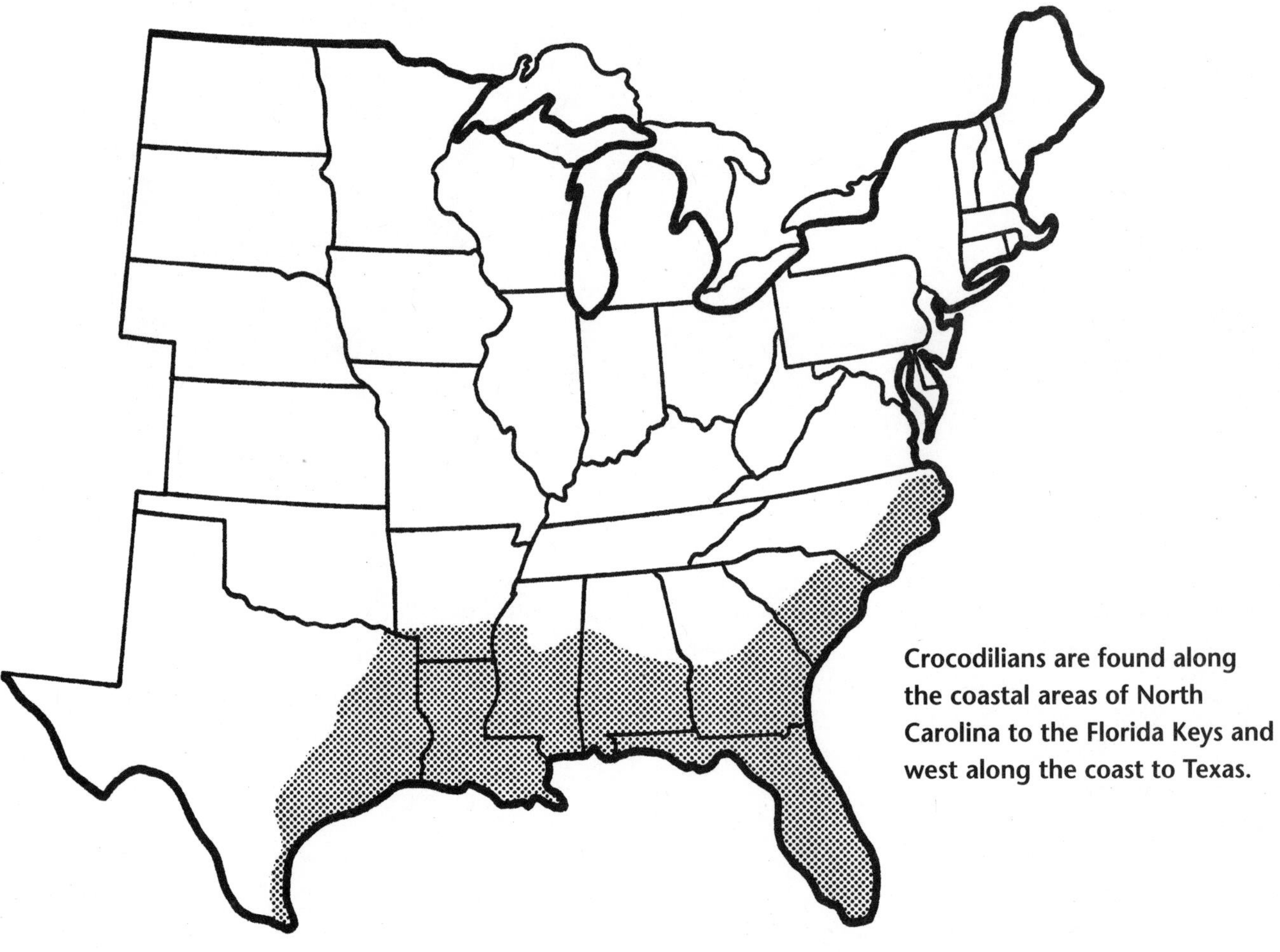

Crocodilians are found along the coastal areas of North Carolina to the Florida Keys and west along the coast to Texas.

The American alligator has been known to reach a length of more than $5\frac{1}{2}$ meters (about 18 feet). This makes the alligator the largest reptile in North America. Until the late 1960s, the alligator population was declining steadily because of illegal hunting practices. However, efforts were made to protect alligators, and these animals are no longer on the endangered species list. Alligators create large dens (holes) before hibernating in the mud for the dry winter months. During droughts, these holes provide a refuge for aquatic animals that would otherwise die.

American crocodiles are often a little smaller than alligators and live in the coastal mangrove forests of southern Florida. Their habitat has been greatly reduced because of coastal building, and their population has declined to well under 1,000. They are included on the growing list of endangered species. Crocodiles can usually be distinguished from alligators by two characteristics. First, most alligators have a broad, rounded snout. Most crocodiles have a narrower snout. Second, the fourth tooth in the lower jaw of crocodiles is visible when the mouth is closed.

Alligator

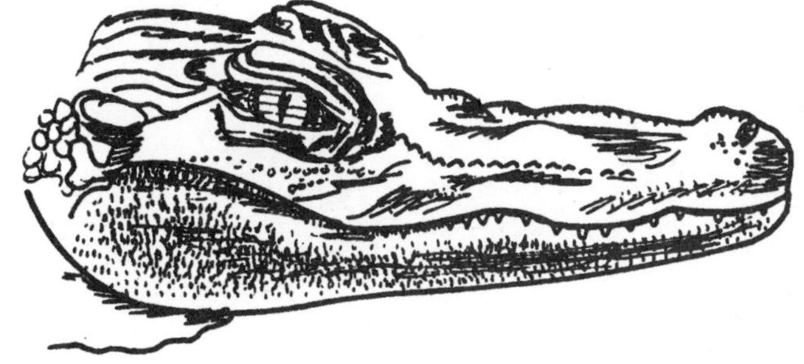

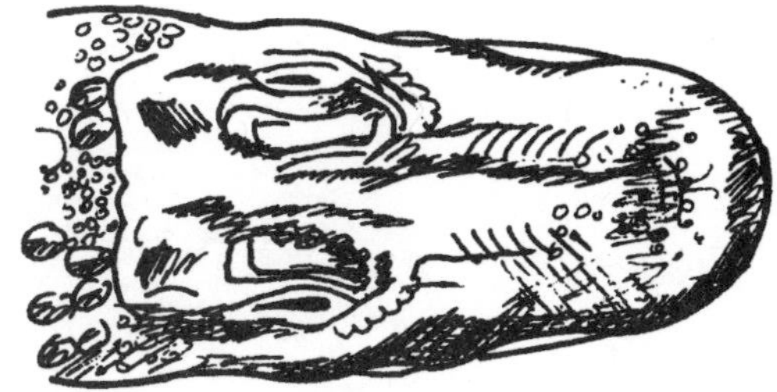

Crocodile

There is a small population of spectacled caimans, which are closely related to alligators and crocodiles, that lives in southern Florida. These animals originally came from Central and South America. Spectacled caimans are a little smaller than crocodiles and alligators. They have been seen in drainage canals, streams, ponds, and marshes. They live in the United States because people purchased them as pets and later released them into the environment. They are named because of a bony ridge in front of their eyes that reminds people of eyeglasses.

Most crocodilians will eat any animal that they can overcome. Young crocodilians eat insects, crustaceans, and fish, but adults usually eat larger prey such as reptiles (including other crocodilians), birds, and mammals. Crocodilians may surprise their victims and knock them off balance. They may also twist their bodies around their prey or lash at them with their powerful tails. The long heads, strong jaws, and cone-shaped teeth of these hunters allow them to hold their prey tightly in their mouths. Although it is not a common occurrence, some crocodilians have killed humans. It is best to avoid alligators and crocodiles that you may see in the wild.

Caiman

Review

Answer the following questions using complete sentences.

1. What is special about a crocodile's heart? ____________________
____

2. What is the largest reptile in North America? ____________________
____

3. Give an example of how a crocodile is different from an alligator.
____
____

4. What type of environment does the American crocodile prefer? ____________________
____
____

5. Where do American crocodiles lay their eggs? ____________________
____
____

6. What is happening to the habitat of the American crocodile?
____
____

7. What do crocodilians eat? ____________________
____
____

8. Which crocodilian is endangered? ____________________
____
____

9. How many species of crocodilians live in the United States? ____________________
____
____

10. How do crocodilians catch their prey? ____________________
____
____

Birds

Unlike most mammals, which often hide away from human sight, birds are seen and heard almost everywhere we go. People have long been fascinated by birds' singing and their ability to fly.

Scientists believe that birds are descended from reptiles. Fossils show that a number of flying reptiles called pterosaurs (winged lizards) existed during the age of dinosaurs. Some of them had wingspans of up to 12 meters (40 feet). This feature probably permitted them to soar for long periods of time. However, no evidence exists to prove that birds are related to pterosaurs.

Modern birds may be related to a birdlike creature called Archaeopteryx ("ancient wing"), which fossil records indicate existed about 150 million years ago. Other fossils show the partial remains of Protoavis ("first bird"), which lived about 225 million years ago. These discoveries have led scientists to believe that reptiles were the ancestors of modern birds. The fact that birds have features similar to those of ancient reptiles supports this theory. For example, birds have a hollow bone structure that is also common to some ancient and modern reptiles. Birds also have scales on their legs, and some species have scales at the base of their bill.

Birds are endothermic (warm-blooded), which means that they have a constant body temperature. This characteristic permits birds to specialize their feeding habits and adapt to different living conditions. From the tropics to the Arctic, birds thrive in a large variety of habitats.

Archaeopteryx

The earth's environment has changed greatly since the first birds appeared. Birds have responded to these changes through constant **adaptation.** In nature, those that adapt to changes in the environment survive, and those that do not adapt usually become extinct. All bird species have made adaptations in the following areas:

- skeletal system—long bones are hollow to reduce body weight
- muscles—powerful muscles attached to the breastbone allow bird to flap its wings
- air sacs—hollow spaces lighten the bird's overall weight; they also help to eliminate excess body heat; this is part of a bird's "air conditioning" system since it cannot sweat

The illustrations below show how birds have adapted to different situations.

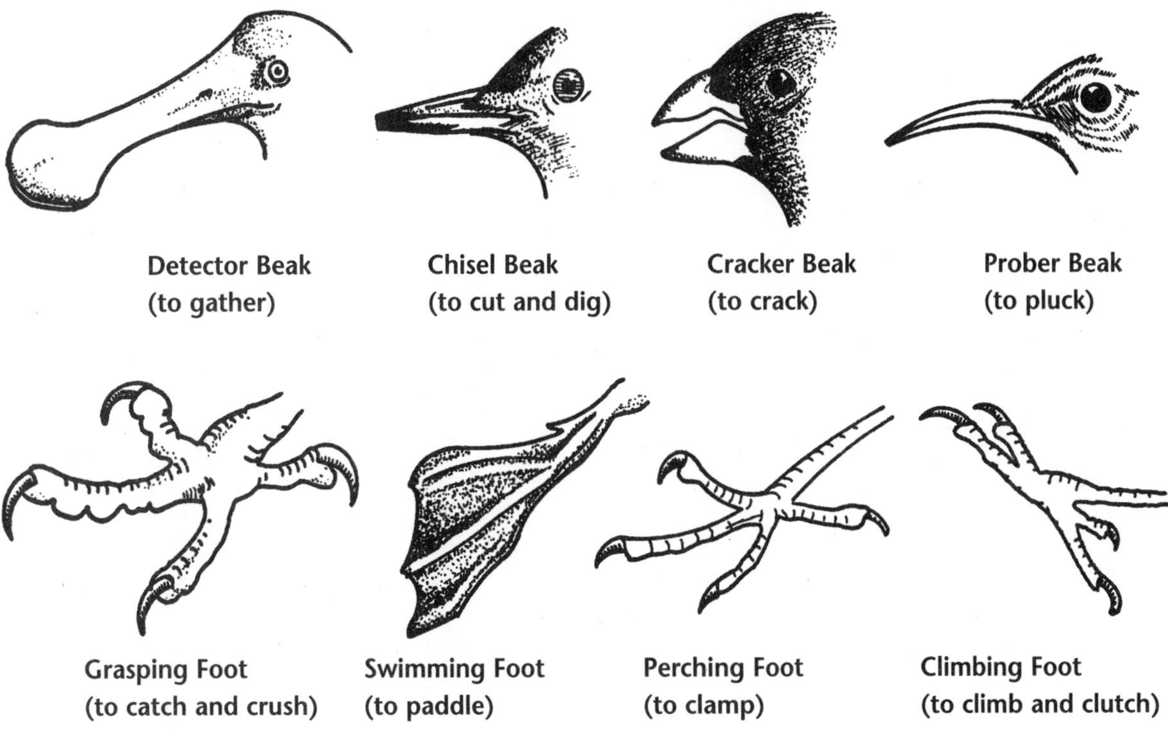

Detector Beak (to gather)
Chisel Beak (to cut and dig)
Cracker Beak (to crack)
Prober Beak (to pluck)

Grasping Foot (to catch and crush)
Swimming Foot (to paddle)
Perching Foot (to clamp)
Climbing Foot (to climb and clutch)

Birds differ from one another in color, size, shape, and flying ability. True flight is a skill possessed only by insects, bats, and birds. Flying fish, flying squirrels, and flying lizards do not actually fly; rather, they just glide through the air. Some birds, such as the ostrich and kiwi, cannot fly either. Among birds, the champion flier is the Arctic tern. Each year this bird flies from the Arctic to Antarctica and back again. Some birds, such as the peregrine falcon, can fly as fast as 339 kilometers (200 miles) per hour. Other birds, like vultures, take advantage of air currents and soar very lazily.

UNIT 3

• Investigate—*Wings vs. Arms* •

Materials
chicken wing
dissecting pan
dissecting kit

Procedures

1. Pull all of the skin off an uncooked chicken wing. Notice how the muscles are attached to different portions of the wing.
2. Carefully cut the tendons that attach each muscle to the bones. As each muscle (the part you eat) is removed, more of the underlying skeleton will be revealed.
3. Examine and compare the structures to the illustrations below.
4. Compare the terms and bone structures of the wing to those of the human arm and hand. Fill in the chart on page 75.

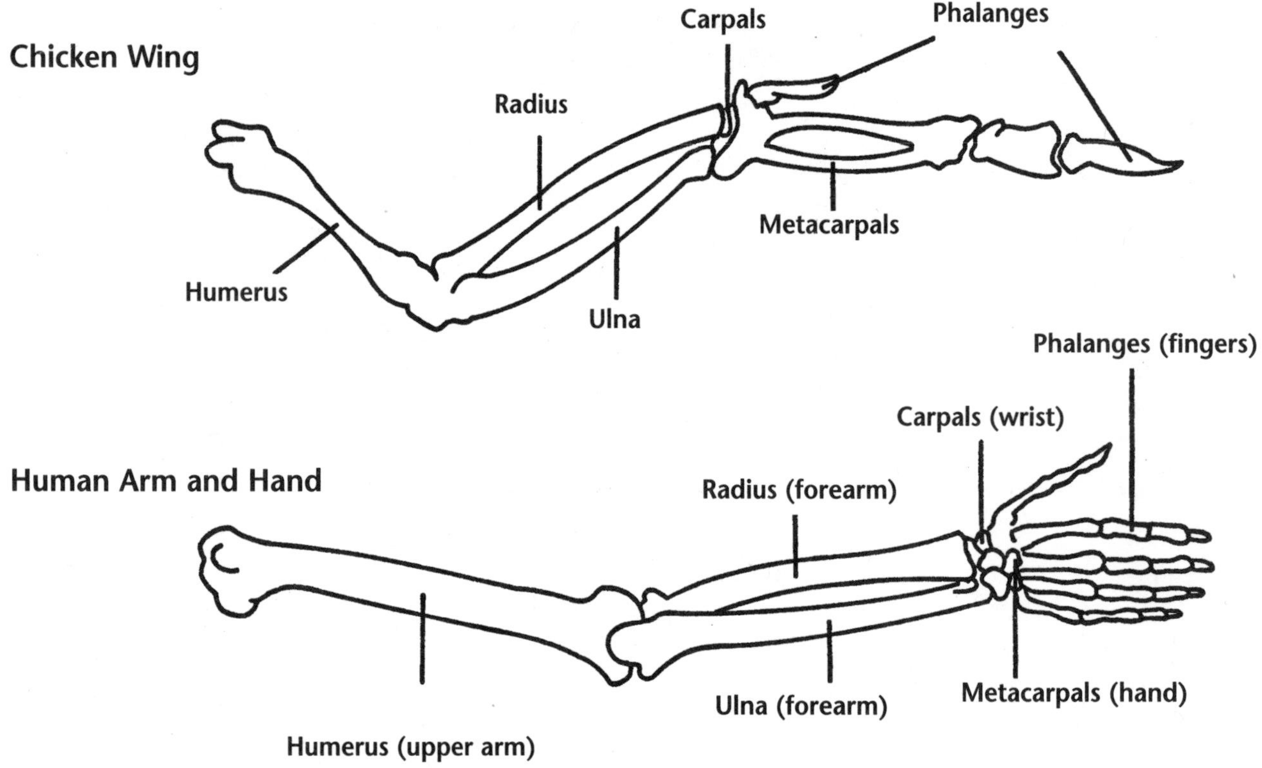

Caution: Be sure to wash your working space, tools, and hands thoroughly with soapy water after completing this investigation.

Human Arm and Chicken Wing Comparison		
Bone	**Similarities**	**Differences**
Humerus		
Radius		
Ulna		
Carpals		
Metacarpals		
Phalanges		

UNIT 3

Birds are the only animals that are covered with feathers. Each bird has different kinds of feathers in different places on its body. Wings have long **primary feathers,** middle-sized **secondary feathers,** and several overlapping **coverts.** Tail feathers extend from the back of the body. Waterfowl have a layer of fluffy **down** beneath their outermost feathers. Some birds have plume feathers, which are used in courtship displays.

Feathers give birds a strong, lightweight, insulating, and streamlined body covering. Birds molt, or shed, their feathers, but they are replaced. Birds will even remove damaged feathers to stimulate growth of healthy replacements.

The growth and development of a feather is very interesting. Each **vane** is made up of barbs (hooks) that grow outward from the shaft or quill. The barbs attach themselves to each other by a series of smaller barbs. If the barbs become separated, the bird can refasten them using its beak.

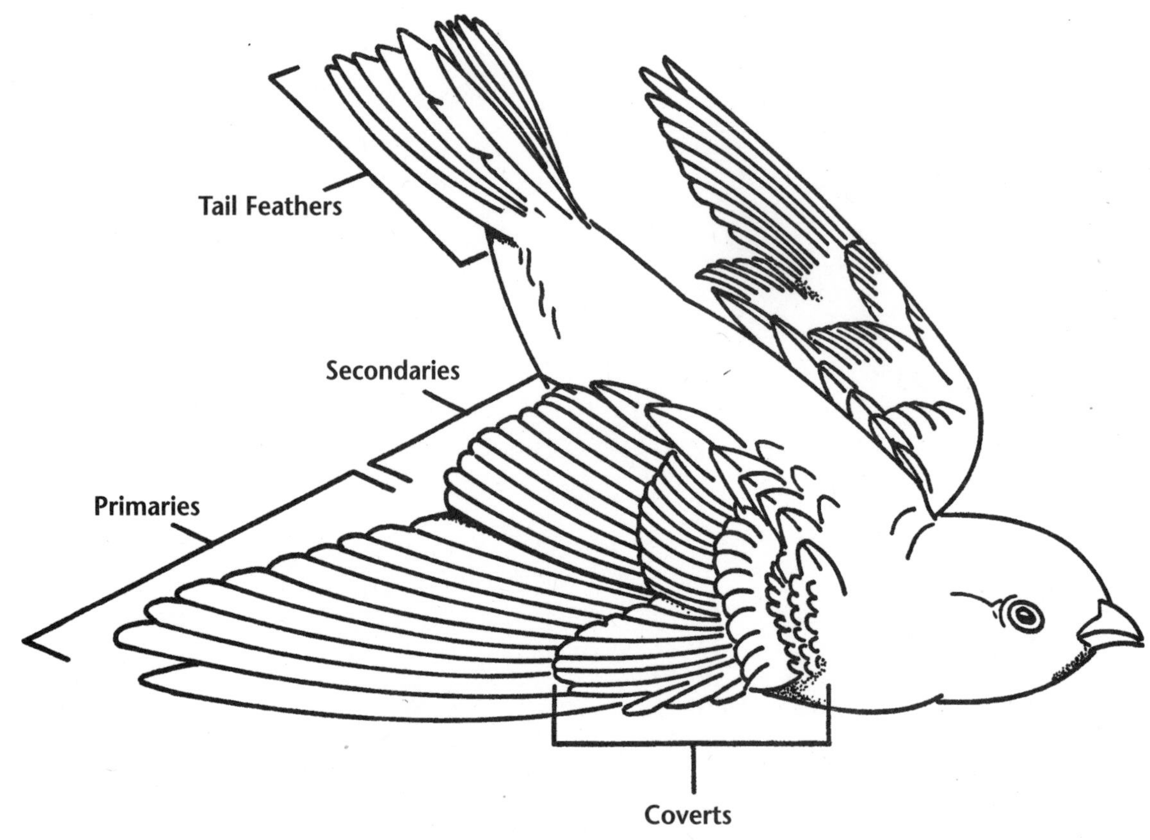

UNIT 3

Classifying Feathers

Search local parks, woodlands, marsh areas, and lawns for feathers of the classifications shown below. Spring and fall are the best times to find feathers. Attach the feathers to this lab paper. The colors and markings, such as spots or stripes, may help you identify the birds the feathers came from. The illustrations in the chart will help you determine what type of feather you have found.

Types of Feathers	
Pattern	**Example**
Pin 	
Covert 	
Down 	
Flight Feather Primary 	
Flight Feather Secondary 	
Tail 	

Review

Complete the following statements with the word from the text that best completes the sentence.

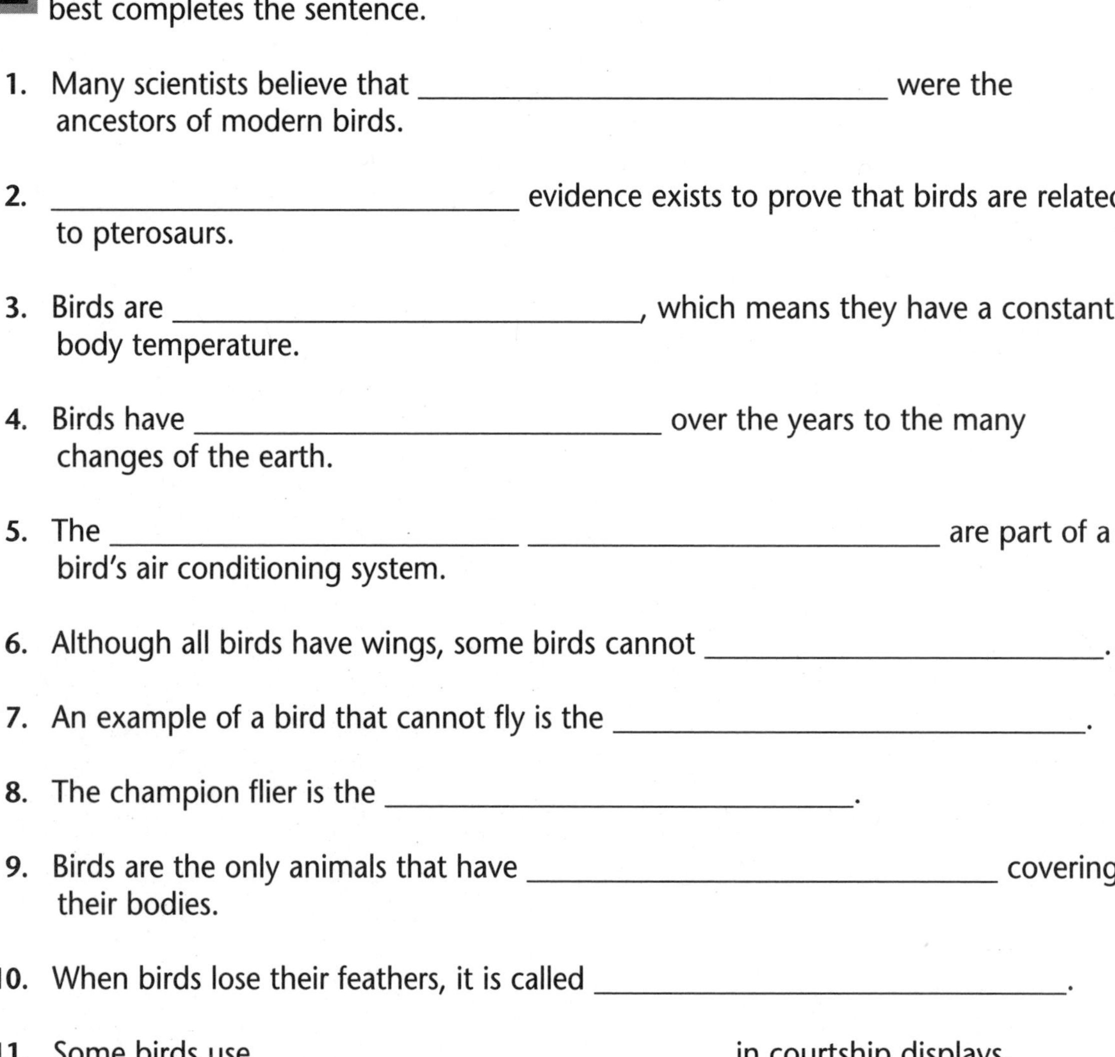

1. Many scientists believe that ____________________ were the ancestors of modern birds.

2. ____________________ evidence exists to prove that birds are related to pterosaurs.

3. Birds are ____________________, which means they have a constant body temperature.

4. Birds have ____________________ over the years to the many changes of the earth.

5. The ____________________ ____________________ are part of a bird's air conditioning system.

6. Although all birds have wings, some birds cannot ____________________.

7. An example of a bird that cannot fly is the ____________________.

8. The champion flier is the ____________________.

9. Birds are the only animals that have ____________________ covering their bodies.

10. When birds lose their feathers, it is called ____________________.

11. Some birds use ____________________ in courtship displays.

12. Birds are similar to reptiles in that they have ____________________ on their legs.

Mammals

Scientists classify mammals as the highest form of animal life. Common characteristics of mammals include:

- mammary glands—produce milk to nourish young
- hair—present at least on part of the body; helps animals regulate body temperature
- endothermic (warm-blooded)—body temperature is nearly constant
- live birth—the exceptions to this are two egg-laying mammals, the platypus and the echidna
- heart—has four chambers
- large brain—allows information to be stored for later use

Mammals have been divided into approximately 4,500 species. They are the most dominant animals on earth today and exist in all parts of the world, including the ocean.

Fossils show that creatures like mammals were on the earth before the dinosaurs. Mammals did not begin to thrive until the end of the age of reptiles, when new feeding niches and habitats became available. Mammals probably survived extinction because their brains were highly developed.

Comparison of Brains in Animals

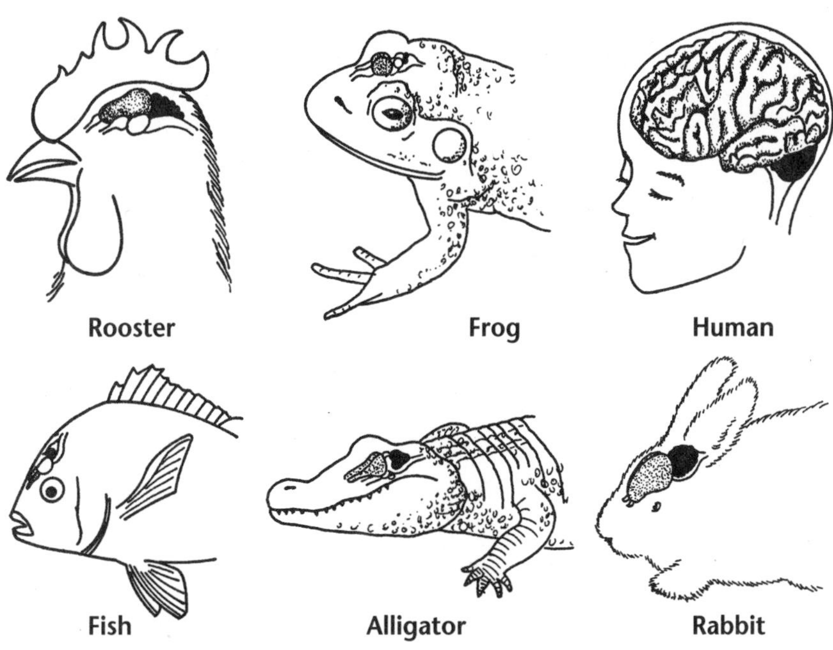

UNIT 3

The brains of mammals vary greatly in size, shape, and level of complexity. Shrews, rats, mice, and rabbits have relatively simple brains compared to the larger, more highly developed brains of dogs, elephants, whales, apes, and humans. The brain allows mammals to store information for later use. It is a remarkable organ that allows **subhuman** animals to solve some problems in their environment.

At the present time, there is no way to measure an animal's thoughts and emotional processes. Each animal's brain has developed to allow the creature to cope with its natural environment. Once domesticated (tamed), many animals are no longer able to function in the wild. They lack the necessary knowledge.

People have domesticated many types of mammals. For example, cats, dogs, guinea pigs, gerbils, hamsters, mice, rats, and squirrels are often kept as pets. Studying pets is very difficult because most people interpret their behavior in human terms and don't recognize the animals' actual behavioral characteristics. Some studies indicate that pets respond to their owners' behaviors, which brings about behavioral changes on their part.

The best way to learn about animal behavior is to buy an animal, such as a mouse, that has a simple set of behaviors. Pages 81–84 contain **ethographs** (charts) in which you can record the behaviors of a mouse.

Answer the following questions in the space provided.

1. What group do scientists classify as the highest form of animal life? ____________________

____

2. Does a mammal's body temperature change? ____________________

____

3. How do mammals feed their young? ____________________

____

4. Where can you find mammals living? ____________________

____

5. What is remarkable about a mammal's brain? ____________________

____

• Investigate—*Animal Behavior* •

A House your mouse in a metal cage or glass or plastic enclosure. Line the floor of the habitat with wood shavings, dry grass, or other absorbent material. At this stage in the observation, house your mouse alone and do not add any toys or containers to the habitat. In the data table below, note how often and for how long each behavior takes place. In the blank spaces, list any additional behaviors that your mouse displays. Record the behaviors of the mouse for five days.

Observation Date and Time **Today's Date:**	**Exercising**	**Exploring**	**Feeding**	**Drinking**	**Resting**	**Fighting**	**Nest Building**	**Face Washing**		
9:00–9:15	M 45 Sec	M 240 Sec / 310 Sec F	M 45 Sec / 30 Sec F	M 10 Sec / 15 Sec F	M 555 Sec / 215 Sec F		30 Sec F	M 5 Sec / 15 Sec F		
10:00–10:15										
11:00–11:15										
12:00–12:15										

Key: **Male = M** **Female = F**

Observation Date and Time Today's Date:	Exercising	Exploring	Feeding	Drinking	Resting	Fighting	Nest Building	Face Washing		
9:00–9:15										
10:00–10:15										
11:00–11:15										
12:00–12:15										

Key: Male = M Female = F

Observation Date and Time Today's Date:	Exercising	Exploring	Feeding	Drinking	Resting	Fighting	Nest Building	Face Washing		
9:00–9:15										
10:00–10:15										
11:00–11:15										
12:00–12:15										

Key: Male = M Female = F

Observation Date and Time Today's Date:	Exercising	Exploring	Feeding	Drinking	Resting	Fighting	Nest Building	Face Washing		
9:00–9:15										
10:00–10:15										
11:00–11:15										
12:00–12:15										

Key: Male = M Female = F

Observation Date and Time Today's Date:	Exercising	Exploring	Feeding	Drinking	Resting	Fighting	Nest Building	Face Washing		
9:00–9:15										
10:00–10:15										
11:00–11:15										
12:00–12:15										

Key: Male = M Female = F

U N I T 3

B After you've made your initial observations, this study can be made more interesting. Make a new environment for the animal by adding an exercise wheel and some cardboard containers. Next, introduce two or more new mice to the habitat. Continue to fill in the data table to determine whether behavior seems more complex in a richer environment. Make four copies of the ethograph on which to record your observations for five days.

Observation Date and Time **Today's Date:**	**Exercising**	**Exploring**	**Feeding**	**Drinking**	**Resting**	**Fighting**	**Nest Building**	**Face Washing**		
9:00–9:15										
10:00–10:15										
11:00–11:15										
12:00–12:15										

Key: Male = M Female = F

C Data tables such as the one above can also be used to study wild animals, but the observations need to be made in the animal's natural environment. This is very challenging and requires much patience. However, it is rewarding to know that the observation was done in a realistic, scientific manner. Design your own ethograph using the table above as a guide. Note: This type of study is not appropriate for studying domestic house cats and dogs because of their complex makeup. You might try to observe hamsters or guinea pigs, or even reptiles such as turtles or lizards.

Mammals

Mammals are divided into three main groups based on how they reproduce. The vast majority of mammals belong to the group called *placentals.* In placental mammals, the mother carries the young inside her body until they have reached a fairly advanced level of development. The period in which the young remain inside the mother is called *gestation.* Placentals with short gestation periods often have young that are blind, hairless, and helpless at birth. When the gestation period is long, the young are alert soon after birth and may have all their hair, and may even be able to walk or run immediately.

Another group of mammals, the *marsupials,* give birth to young that are tiny and poorly developed. Immediately after birth, the young attach themselves to the mother's nipples, which in most species are in a pouch on the stomach. The young remain there until they develop more completely. Most marsupial mammals live in Australia and on surrounding islands. Australian marsupials include kangaroos, koala bears, and wombats. The common opossum is the only marsupial species native to the United States.

The only mammals that do not bear live young are the *monotremes.* The duck-billed platypus and two species of echidna (spiny anteater) are the only known monotremes in existence. After mating, female monotremes lay eggs. The platypus lays one to three eggs in a burrow, while female echidnas deposit a single egg in a pouch on their stomach. After hatching, young monotremes complete their development inside the burrow or, in the case of the echidnas, inside the mother's pouch.

Use the information to answer the questions.

1. How are mammals grouped? ______________________________

____

2. What are the three main groups of mammals? ______________________________

____

3. How are monotremes different from marsupials and placentals? ______________________________

____

4. What are three kinds of marsupials? ______________________________

____

5. How do young marsupials differ from young placentals at birth? ______________________________

____

6. What is the period in which a mother carries her young inside her body? ______________________________

____

UNIT 3

Review

■ Complete the puzzle.

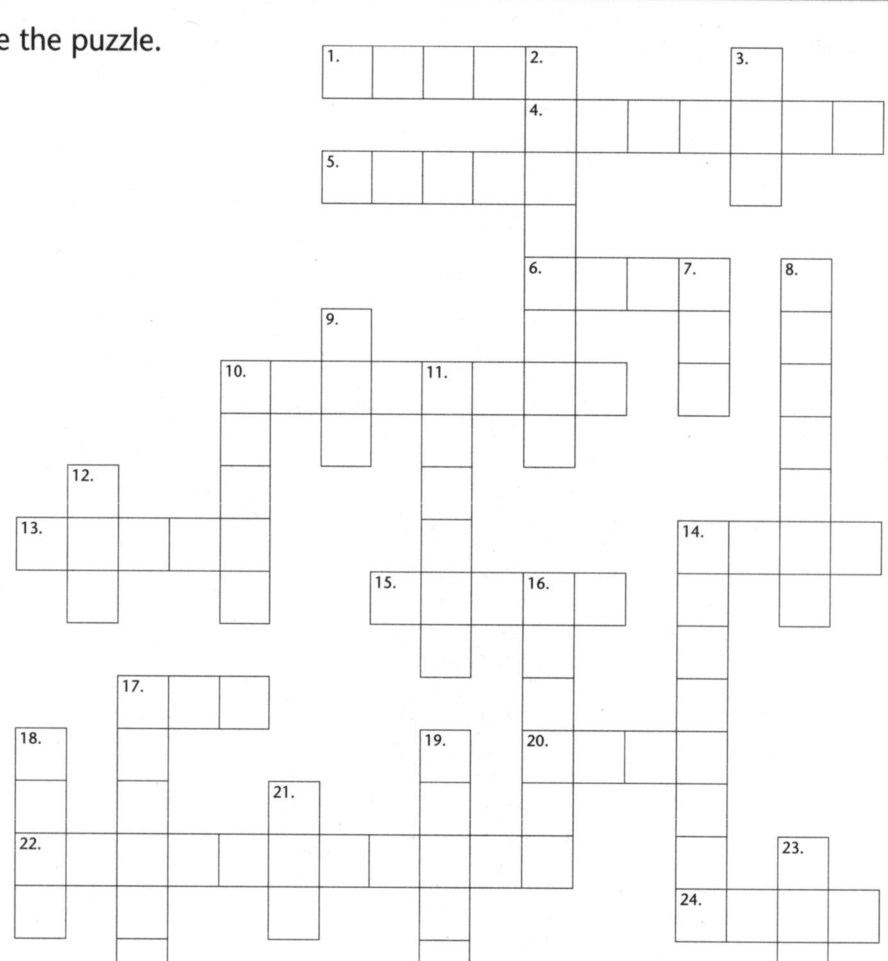

Across Clues

1. small rodent that likes cheese
4. large, spotted, wild cat
5. largest animal on earth
6. trait that all mammals have
10. small, striped ground squirrel
13. four-legged riding animal
14. fish-eating mammal with flippers
15. striped horselike animal
17. only flying mammal
20. "Smokey ______"
22. total surroundings
24. "king of the jungle"

Down Clues

2. largest land animal
3. popular household pet
7. long-tailed rodent larger than a mouse
8. an animal's natural environment
9. farm animal that we get ham from
10. desert animal with a hump
11. common primate
12. known for clever nature
14. nut-gathering mammal that builds nests in trees
16. common member of the hare family
17. known for building dams on rivers
18. the males of this woodland animal have antlers
19. animal that we get wool from
21. farm animal that we get milk from
23. first animal tamed by people

Review Unit 3

REVIEW

A Answer the following questions. You may refer to the lessons.

1. List three characteristics that are unique to chordates.

2. How is it possible for humans to qualify as chordates on all three of these characteristics?

3. What large group of extinct reptiles once lived in the Mesozoic Period?

4. What four groups of animals are classified as reptiles?

5. Name three characteristics of reptiles.

6. List four reasons why feathers are useful to birds.

7. Write the sentence in the text that indicates that mammals were on earth a very long time ago.

8. Write the sentence that suggests that domestication places limitations on some mammals.

REVIEW

B Circle "T" if the statement is true or "F" if the statement is false.

1. T F Turtles have gone through many body changes over the years.
2. T F A turtle has no protection against natural hazards.
3. T F Turtles have growth rings on the plates of their shells.
4. T F Turtles migrate or travel south for the winter.
5. T F Scientists believe baby turtles know what to eat because of "chemical imprinting."
6. T F A snake can only eat prey that is smaller than the diameter of its head.
7. T F Copperhead snakes inject a venom into the prey's blood that can cause quick death to a small animal.
8. T F Snakes are of no benefit to humans.
9. T F Snakes use their teeth to hold their prey.
10. T F All snakes swallow their prey whole.
11. T F Coral snakes are not a major threat to humans because their fangs are small.
12. T F Snakes face no danger when they attack their prey.
13. T F Most snakes have one lung.
14. T F All snakes are dangerous to humans.
15. T F Some snakes will eat other snakes.

C Match the terms describing a human arm to the similar part of a chicken wing.

________	**1.** phalanges	**a.** wrist
________	**2.** ulna	**b.** upper arm
________	**3.** metacarpals	**c.** fingers
________	**4.** humerus	**d.** hand
________	**5.** carpals	**e.** forearm

End-of-Book Test

TEST

Circle the letter that correctly completes each statement.

1. The word ________ refers to the chemical processes that change food into energy.
   a. eating
   b. respiration
   c. metabolism
   d. molting
2. The earthworm's niche is ________.
   a. controlling the mosquito population
   b. burrowing
   c. providing food to all forms of aquatic life
   d. secreting mucus
3. An earthworm's eggs are ________.
   a. encased in a mucus cocoon
   b. wrapped in a silk cocoon
   c. preyed upon by larger animals
   d. protected by a leathery shell
4. The ________ group contains more species than all other animal groups combined.
   a. Crustacean
   b. Mammal
   c. Arthropod
   d. Beetle
5. All spiders ________.
   a. are herbivores
   b. spin webs
   c. are harmful to people
   d. produce silken fibers
6. Mites are similar to spiders in that they ________.
   a. have eight legs
   b. all eat meat
   c. have both male and female reproductive organs
   d. spin webs
7. Scorpions are unlike spiders in that they ________.
   a. inject venom into their prey
   b. can be found in warm and cool climates
   c. have eight legs
   d. bear their young alive
8. Crustaceans have been on earth ________.
   a. since the dinosaurs ruled the planet
   b. for about 12 billion years
   c. as long as humans
   d. for about 600 million years
9. Crustaceans ________,so it is difficult for them to live on land.
   a. breathe with gills
   b. are allergic to sunshine
   c. rely on plankton for food
   d. need a stable saltwater environment
10. The niche of the crayfish is to ________.
    a. keep the environment clean and thin out the population of weak animals
    b. provide humans with food
    c. control the population of destructive animal species
    d. enrich the soil
11. Millipedes may ________ when handled.
    a. sting
    b. bite
    c. curl up defensively
    d. release toxic substances
12. Unlike millipedes, centipedes ________.
    a. have one hundred legs
    b. have two pair of legs per body section
    c. eat meat
    d. reproduce by laying eggs
13. The largest group of arthropods are the ________.
    a. crustaceans
    b. earthworms
    c. ants
    d. insects
14. Humans use pesticides because ________.
    a. all insects are harmful to humans
    b. there are not enough predators to control some insect populations
    c. it enhances the quality of the food we grow
    d. insects cause damage to clothing and wood

TEST

15. The niche of an insect in nature is _______.
   a. to control the plant population
   b. to keep the environment clean
   c. determined by what kind of food it eats
   d. not helpful to humans
16. Insects use their antennae to _______.
   a. gather sensory information
   b. reproduce
   c. inject venom
   d. spread disease
17. Every adult insect has _______.
   a. wings
   b. three pairs of legs
   c. simple eyes
   d. two body sections
18. Complete metamorphosis _______.
   a. consists of four stages
   b. happens whenever the insect has outgrown its exoskeleton
   c. indicates that newborn insects look like their parents
   d. occurs in all arthropods
19. The digestive process of an insect takes place in the gullet, crop, and _______.
   a. spiracles
   b. stomach
   c. gizzard
   d. pupa
20. All insects are cold-blooded, which means that _______.
   a. they can stay underground for long periods
   b. they are more advanced creatures than the crustaceans
   c. they don't have sensory organs
   d. their body temperature varies with that of the air
21. The most common type of insect is the _______.
   a. firefly
   b. ladybug
   c. beetle
   d. earthworm
22. The beetle molts after __________.
   a. two weeks
   b. adult organs form
   c. the adult beetle emerges
   d. the legs fall off
23. The colors on the wings of moths and butterflies are _______.
   a. caused by scales on the surface of the wings
   b. a protective device
   c. used to create paint pigments
   d. similar
24. One difference between moths and butterflies is that moths _______.
   a. have stalklike antennae
   b. have two pairs of wings
   c. undergo complete metamorphosis
   d. keep their wings outstretched when they land
25. Social insects _______.
   a. mate for life
   b. live in colonies
   c. all perform the same functions
   d. live in the ground
26. Every ant colony must have _______.
   a. a queen
   b. an anthill
   c. a honeycomb
   d. slaves
27. Worker ants _______.
   a. mate with the queen
   b. tear off the wings of the queen after she has mated
   c. protect the nest and care for the queen
   d. kill male ants after mating
28. The queen bee is fertilized _______.
   a. every three to five years
   b. during a nuptial flight
   c. by worker bees
   d. by another queen bee

29. Bees communicate with each other about food sources by _______.
   a. dancing
   b. a series of high-pitched sounds
   c. leaving a trail of scent
   d. chemical imprinting

30. Termites are somewhat similar to _______.
   a. ants
   b. grubs
   c. cockroaches and grasshoppers
   d. spiders

31. Termites are different from ants and bees in that _______.
   a. they are social insects
   b. only one female reproduces
   c. workers take care of the queen
   d. both a royal male and female live in each colony

32. Soldier termites must usually _______.
   a. leave the colony when others are born
   b. fight to the death
   c. tear off their wings
   d. be fed by workers because they are unable to feed themselves

33. The function of a male wasp is to _______.
   a. build the nest
   b. find a location for the nest
   c. mate with the queen
   d. make paper by chewing soft wood

34. Most wasps are herbivores but they _______.
   a. kill insects that invade their territory
   b. hunt insects and feed the prey to their young
   c. will eat dead or dying insects
   d. feast on spiders during mating season

35. Features that characterize members of the chordate group are a tubular nerve cord, a notochord, and _______.
   a. a highly developed brain
   b. endothermic blood temperature
   c. external ears
   d. gill slits

36. The most advanced kind of chordates are the _______.
   a. vertebrates
   b. reptiles
   c. able to reproduce on land
   d. in danger of extinction

37. Amphibians' reproductive cycles _______.
   a. must take place in an aquatic environment
   b. were the first to allow for the birth of live young
   c. are three to five weeks long
   d. are ambisexual

38. Amphibians are poikilothermic, which means that _______.
   a. they must all hibernate for part of the year
   b. they must reproduce in an aquatic environment
   c. they begin life as herbivores but become carnivores
   d. their body temperature changes with that of the air

39. Salamanders differ from lizards in that they _______.
   a. have no scales, claws, or tongues
   b. are cold-blooded
   c. have no scales, claws, or external ear openings
   d. are carnivorous

40. Frogs differ from toads in that they _______.
   a. have no scales, claws, or warts
   b. have a more developed reproductive cycle
   c. eat insects that are harmful to humans
   d. have longer, more powerful legs

TEST

41. Scientists have studied the fossil remains of dinosaurs and found ________.
   a. they died out because they had no predators
   b. that their hollow bones were what allowed for their great size
   c. that the average-sized dinosaur was about 130 centimeters (4 feet) tall
   d. they lived in aquatic environments
42. Reptiles are more advanced than amphibians because they ________.
   a. are not dependent on an aquatic environment to reproduce
   b. are carnivorous
   c. are social animals
   d. don't need to hibernate in the winter
43. Fossil evidence shows that turtles ________.
   a. have changed greatly over the years
   b. had a spinal chord before any other animal did
   c. have outer shells made out of flattened ribs
   d. have been on the earth for over 200 million years
44. Some turtles are in danger of extinction because ________.
   a. their young have soft shells for several years
   b. they can't protect themselves from their growing number of predators
   c. their habitat is being destroyed by human beings
   d. they can't adapt to the earth's changing climate
45. The jaw of a snake is unique because it ________.
   a. is strong enough to kill small mammals immediately
   b. can stretch wide enough to swallow prey larger than the diameter of the snake's head
   c. is the snake's main hunting tool
   d. varies greatly from species to species
46. Copperheads, coral snakes, cottonmouths, and rattlesnakes are all ________.
   a. capable of swallowing their prey whole
   b. in danger of becoming extinct
   c. found in damp, humid regions of the United States
   d. venomous
47. The majority of North American lizards are ________.
   a. venomous
   b. herbivores
   c. active during the day
   d. dangerous to humans
48. Crocodilians are different from other reptiles because they ________.
   a. have a four-chambered heart like birds and mammals
   b. can be found along coastal regions in the southern United States
   c. are dangerous to humans
   d. reproduce by laying eggs with a leathery shell
49. One difference between alligators and crocodiles is that ________.
   a. crocodiles are larger than alligators
   b. crocodiles have longer teeth than alligators
   c. the alligator population is no longer on the endangered species list
   d. alligators lay their eggs in decaying vegetation
50. When the crocodile's mouth is closed ________.
   a. the fourth tooth of the lower jaw is visible
   b. it is difficult to distinguish between it and an alligator
   c. it cannot breathe underwater
   d. it is at rest

51. Fossil evidence has led scientists to believe that ________.
   a. birds have been on the earth for over 265 million years
   b. early birds had hollow bones
   c. reptiles capable of true flight existed during the age of the dinosaurs
   d. reptiles were ancestors to modern birds

52. Most birds have ________.
   a. hollow bones, powerful flight muscles, and air sacs
   b. chisel beaks to cut up and dig for food
   c. feet that allow them to clamp and ulnas that allow them to fly
   d. plume feathers used during mating

53. When birds molt, or shed, their feathers, ________.
   a. it means that spring is coming
   b. they are becoming adults
   c. they are simulating the behavior of their reptile ancestors
   d. the feathers are replaced

54. Bird feathers have barbs, which ________.
   a. act as a protective device
   b. hook onto other feathers
   c. cannot be reattached once they become separated
   d. lay beneath the outermost feathers

55. Birds are unique in the animal kingdom because of their ________.
   a. four-chambered heart
   b. ability to fly
   c. feathers
   d. reproductive cycle

56. Scientists believe that mammals are ________.
   a. ancestors of the early reptiles
   b. the only warm-blooded animals
   c. the earliest inhabitants of earth
   d. the highest form of animal life

57. Mammals are able to nurse their young because ________.
   a. they have mammary glands, which produce milk
   b. have a more highly developed brain
   c. do not lay eggs
   d. have adapted to their environment

58. Although most mammals give birth to live young, some mammals ________.
   a. have mammary glands which produce milk
   b. care for their young after birth
   c. lay eggs
   d. develop through the process of metamorphosis

59. Large, well-developed brains allow mammals to ________.
   a. nurse their young
   b. store information for later use
   c. use oxygen more efficiently
   d. use other animals for energy

60. Once domesticated, many mammals may ________.
   a. not be able to survive in a wild environment
   b. live much longer lives
   c. be able to store greater amounts of information
   d. learn more quickly

Glossary

A

adaptation: a change that makes plants or animals better suited to their environment

algae: a plant that may exist as a single-celled or a many-celled organism. These plants are found in watery or wet surroundings.

arachnids: group of arthropods that includes spiders, scorpions, mites, and ticks

associative nerve: a nerve cell responsible for the transfer of a message from the sensory nerve to the motor nerve.

B

bacteria: microscopic creatures. Some bacteria cause disease and others are necessary for certain processes.

break down: to rot or to change a substance into smaller, more usable parts

brood: the offspring of an animal

burrowing: to progress through the earth by digging and tunneling

C

captivity: held in confinement

carnivore: meat eater

cartilage: a tough, elastic, connective tissue that may form a skeleton, or a protective and supportive tissue that may be part of a skeleton

casting: that which is thrown off or, in the case of an earthworm, the mixture of soil and waste products that passes out of the digestive tract

cell: a small, living unit of protoplasm; a chamber or compartment

cellular: like a cell, or consisting of many cells

cellulose: a complex chemical compound that makes up the cell walls of plants

chemical compounds: molecules composed of elements in specific proportions

chrysalis: the protective case or shell that encloses a developing butterfly between the pupa and adult stage

colony: a group of organisms working together

commerce: the official trading, buying, or selling of merchandise

complete metamorphosis: consisting of four stages of development—egg, larva, pupa, and adult

compound eye: an eye structure that consists of many lenses each focusing a portion of an overall image onto a series of nerves which then relays that message to the animal's brain

coverts: feathers covering the base of the quills of the wing and tail feathers of a bird

crop: an enlargement of the gullet

D

defensive: self-protective

diameter: the length of a straight line through the center of an object

dorsal blood vessel: tube that carries blood away from the heart in an earthworm

down: the fluffy feather layer found beneath the outermost feathers of some birds

E

embryonic: an early stage of development before birth

encased: enclosed, sealed in

enriched: increased in value; made more fertile

ensure: to guarantee an outcome

environment: total surroundings

esophagus: the part of the digestive tract between the mouth and stomach or similar organ

ethograph: a chart of behaviors

GLOSSARY

expand: to get larger

extinction: the process of becoming nonexistent

F

fertilized: describes the state in which the male cell (sperm) is joined with the female cell (egg) to produce young

food chain: the transfer of energy from plants to plant eaters (herbivores) and from plant eaters to a series of meat eaters (carnivores)

fossil record: the total preserved remains of life forms that have existed on the earth

G

gizzard: an enlarged muscular region of the digestive tract, useful in grinding foods

gullet: tube leading from the mouth to the stomach, also called the esophagus

H

habitat: the place where a plant or animal species lives and grows

haphazard: random, disorganized

herbivore: plant eater

hibernation: the dormant or resting state in which some animals pass the winter

humus: decayed plant material found in the soil

I

incomplete metamorphosis: consisting of three stages of development: egg, nymph, and adult

incubate: to provide a favorable environment in which to hatch eggs

infertile: not capable of having offspring

infest: to overrun in great number

inhabitant: a resident of a habitat

instinctive: an inborn habit; a behavior that is known and unlearned

intestine: organ in which digestion takes place

L

larva: the immature free-living form of an animal

life form: an example of an organism that carries out processes such as reproduction, digestion, respiration, and growth, which are essential for life

M

mammal: a class of vertebrate animals characterized as possessing hair, being warm-blooded, and having the capacity to nurse their young

membrane: a thin, flexible coating

motor nerve: a nerve cell that controls the action of muscle tissue

mucous gland: an organ that secretes a slimy fluid for protective purposes

mucus cocoon: a protective covering around the egg mass of the earthworm

N

neurotoxin: a chemical that interferes with the normal functioning of nervous tissue

nuptial flight: the mating flight of the queen bee

nymph: the immature form of an insect that resembles the adult of a species

O

offensive: unpleasant, such as the odor given off by a skunk; related to an attack

P

paralyze: to bring about the loss of muscle activity

parasite: an organism that lives off another living form

plankton: the usually microscopic animal and plant life found floating in aquatic environments

pollinate: the act of transferring pollen to the stigma of a flower

GLOSSARY

predator: hunter

prey: an animal that is being hunted

primary feathers: flight feathers at the wing-tip

processes: a series of changes that occur in a particular way to bring about a specific result

pupa: the developmental stage that occurs between larva and adult

pupate: to enter the pupal stage of development

R

reproductives: the only members of a termite nest that are capable of mating and producing offspring

rigid: firm, inflexible

royal jelly: a creamy compound rich in protein and minerals that is made by young worker bees and fed to all grubs for a few days. Continued feeding will result in the development of the rival queens.

S

secondary feathers: similar to primary feathers, but located along the trailing edge of the wing

segmented: divided into or made up of sections

sensory nerve: a nerve that responds to a stimulus such as touch, taste, smell, heat, or pressure

simple eye: an eye having a single lens

skeleton: the hard, supporting framework of an animal's body

species: a distinct type of life form that usually breeds only with others of its kind

spinneret: the gland from which a spider emits the silklike substance that is sometimes used in web making

stereomicroscope: a microscope that has a set of optics for each eye and makes the object appear in three dimensions

subhuman: developmentally below the human species

T

toxic substance: a poison

trait: a quality or characteristic

V

vane: the web or flat, expanded part of a feather

venom: a naturally produced chemical substance injected by bite or sting and used for protection or for capturing prey

ventral blood vessel: the tube through which blood returns to heart after it has circulated through the body of an earthworm

vertebrate: any animal having a backbone of bone or cartilage